That Perfect Stitch

SECOND EDITION

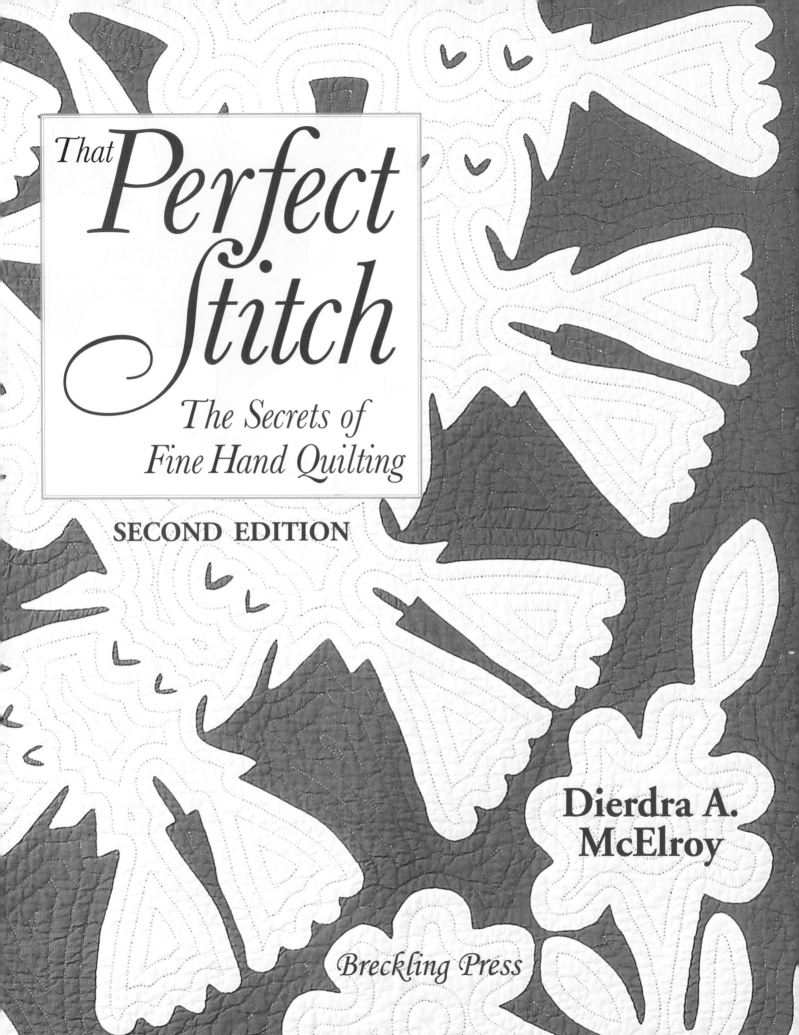

That Perfect Stitch

The Secrets of Fine Hand Quilting

SECOND EDITION

Dierdra A. McElroy

Breckling Press

This Second Edition
of *That Perfect Stitch*
is based on the
original book by
Roxanne McElroy

Library of Congress Cataloging-in-Publication Data

Library of Congress
Cataloging-in-Publication Data is available from the Library of Congress.

This book was set in Garamond and Myriad
Editorial direction by Anne Knudsen
Quilt photography by Sharon Risedorph, San Francisco, unless otherwise credited
Photographs of quilts in settings and quilting tools by Sharon Hoogstraten, Chicago

Published by Breckling Press
283 N. Michigan St, Elmhurst, IL 60126

Printed and bound in Hong Kong. Developed and produced in United States.
International Standard Book Number (ISBN 13): 978-1-933308-27-2

I would like to dedicate this book to my father, Jeff McElroy. He has endured three generations of quilters in his life. My mother Roxanne, myself, and my daughter Victoria. He has been the solid steady rock to our creative disasters and successes. Without him, this book would not be possible.

My love, admiration, and gratitude goes out to another special man, a novelist known to me as Ari. He lovingly pushed me through writer's block, and encouraged, supported, and motivated me to continue writing, despite everything.

CONTENTS

Balloons over New Mexico. Made by Roxanne McElroy.
A champagne glass design fills this quilt to the borders.

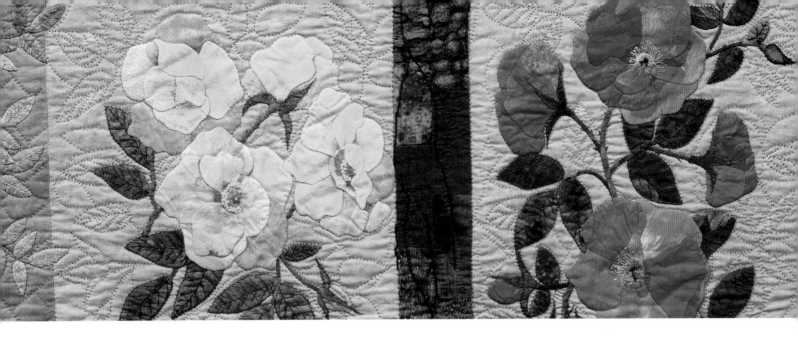

In My Dreams: A Self Portrait. Made by Roxanne McElroy.
This portrait shows just how much you can do with channel appliqué! My mother used various quilting techniques, including echo-quilting along the lines, freehand quilting in the sky, and little circles on the bodice. She left the face and other areas of skin free of quilting stitches.

My sincere thanks goes out to all the students who have attended my classes over the years. I have learned something new from each and every one of you. I am ever grateful to the quilters who have allowed their quilts to be photographed for my book. The world deserves to see your beautiful works of art! The infinite patience of Grace Frame Company, Colonial Needle Company, Hoffman California Fabrics, and Superior Threads must also be recognized. They have tolerated an endless number of questions and shared their individual areas of expertise. I would like to thank all the hand-quilting teachers out there who strive to share the time-honored tradition of making quilts by hand. My daughter Victoria has helped me and supported me during years of traveling, even though it meant missing out on birthdays and Halloween. Thank you, and I love you dearly. Without input and support from all these people and organizations, it would have been difficult to research this book. You have all helped quilters the world over achieve That Perfect Stitch!

My mother, Roxanne McElroy, was always larger than life. She never began a hobby with a simple project. Instead, she jumped in at the deep end, with projects that were challenging even for skilled artists. I sometimes think she could have been a scientist because the question "Why?" was always on her lips about everything she touched. She wanted to know why things worked or did not work, and never settled for simple answers. Her gregariousness and happiness were a contagion from which no one was immune. Hundreds of people have told me in confidence that Roxanne was the biggest motivator in their quilting and had a huge impact on their

Tiare de Tahiti. Made by Roxanne McElroy.
The national flower of Tahiti is quilted in ¹/₂ inch (1.2 cm) echo.

personal lives. She elicited people's self-confidence in such a positive way that careers were changed, marriages saved, and independence won.

Sadly, my mother passed away on April 13, 1997. We were at the first annual World Quilts & Textile show in Pasadena, California. She passed peacefully, although unexpectedly, in her sleep. The previous evening Roxanne had been honored to contribute to the first world panel of quilting teachers. The history, future, trends, and state of quilting in more than 10 nations was shared and discussed in a panel format. Roxanne felt this was a huge success, both politically and artistically.

Roxanne's never-ending quest for answers to her questions about quilting products made her a leading authority on the tools quilters use. She taught a class that was internationally known, in which she shared her research and her talents. Her unique ability to break difficult tasks down into separate manageable steps enabled all of her students to succeed. Many left her class quilting 14 stitches to the inch! I personally felt that her class had come into such demand that she could not possibly go everywhere to teach it. Writing a book would help her reach more quilters. Over the previous five years, several publishers had invited her to write a book, so I went and talked to them. When I found the company that could do her art justice, I took their representatives over to her and introduced them. Of course, I did not tell her that I had already told them she would do the book!

While she was writing, Roxanne complained that she spent more time at the computer than at her quilt frame. She complained that there were already hundreds of quilting books on the market (though very few were dedicated to hand quilting). But, she did it! Sadly, Roxanne left this world one week before getting to see the cover of her new book, *That Perfect Stitch*. I became more determined than ever that her work and ideas be published and made available to quilters. Fortunately, my mother taught me everything she knew, and I, too, had been teaching on the national circuit for a few years. I finished the last bit of the book as she would have wanted it, and I intend to continue her research and share her ideas and talents with the world.

Since the publication of the first edition, the quilting industry has undergone major changes, as manufacturers strive to improve the quality of their hand quilting fabrics and as quilters work to achieve That Perfect Stitch. Every chapter of this book has been updated to respond to those changes and to share new information and techniques with you. I have included more information on fabric selection and introduced a new tool, the ROSE, that will help you determine the thread count of each new fabric before you buy it. The batting chart that so many readers found helpful in the original book has now been expanded to include newer brands and to provide more extensive information on the suitability of each batt to your quilting projects. Similarly, updated information on threads, thimbles, markers and more will bring you up to date with every product you need to improve your quilting stitch. In response to questions from students around the country, I have also reworked our materials on stitching technique, helping you understand and learn how to quilt more beautifully by hand. It is my hope that this new edition will continue Roxanne's legacy for a new generation of quilters.

My mother was my best friend, confidante, and business partner. She was truly the strongest woman I have ever known. She touched so many lives and always carried her own personal party with her everywhere she went. I love you, Mom!

Dierdra A. McElroy

Childhood at my house was a blast! My mother and I tried just about every arts and crafts project possible. We tried oil painting, macramé, knitting, beading, cross-stitch, pottery, baking, photography, among others. And we didn't limit ourselves to beginner projects. For instance, when we took up crochet, our first project was a banquet table cloth! We were best friends and partners in crime.

At age 11, I was living in Tahiti. At Christmastime, my Tahitian nanny/housekeeper gave my family a beautiful Tahitian bedspread, called a Tifaifai.

La Fusiere (**The Fern**). Made by Roxanne McElroy.
This is one of several Tifaifai my mother made in Tahiti, before she learned the quilting stitch. Once we both learned to quilt, we transformed several of those Tifaifai into quilt tops.

Designed for tropical climates, Tifaifai are similar to Hawaiian quilts, with one notable difference—Tifaifai are not quilted at all. They are made from lightweight fabric, intricately appliquéd, and simply hemmed around the edges to form a summer spread. My mother and I made several Tifaifai while we lived in Tahiti. We used them on the beds and laundered them weekly along with the sheets. In 1980 we moved back to the United States, and the Tifaifai were put away in a closet and forgotten.

Several years later, I was a college student at Texas A&M University, studying Biomedical Science. While my life was hectic, my mother felt deserted and alone. She joined a group that hoped to raise funds by making a quilt to raffle. There were a handful of women ready to teach my mother a craft that was new to her. Within an hour, it was obvious that quilting was something my mother was very good at. The women were amazed at her abilities and went so far as to lie on the floor under the quilt frame to stare at her stitches. A few minutes later, they were asking my mother—the newest quilter among them—for instruction! Immediately she found she had yet another skill—explaining exactly what she was doing with her hands in words quilters could understand.

My mother's excitement at this new-found craft was evident in her phone calls to me. She realized that she already had over a half-dozen quilt tops in the form of the forgotten Tifaifai from Tahiti. Within months, she had designed Tifaifai patterns of her own and offered them for sale. Within a year of making her first stitches in 1987, she had quilted a quilt for hire, taught her first class, and held her first lecture.

During that whirlwind year, my mother began to notice that her natural quilting ability was not enough to achieve a fine quilting stitch. There were other factors that affected the quality of her stitches. We began a quest to discover why she could quilt 15 stitches per inch on one project but not nearly that many on another. Texas A&M had taught me how to have a questioning mind and how to conduct research. Instinctively, I began to look at all the factors directly involved in quilting, noticing how they affected the stitch. Our research led us down a very interesting path—a path down which I hope you will follow as you read this book.

Together, my mother and I analyzed each and every tool used in the craft of quilting—from needle and thread to batting and cloth. In addition, we developed tools of our own that help quilters improve their stitching. As her work became known to the quilting community, the demand for my mother's time kept her fully booked, and she spent half of every month traveling around the country. Once I graduated college and took my first steps in the job market, I stayed behind the scenes in my mother's quilting business, helping with her research, teaching, and writing. When she became too busy to cope on her own,

I came on board to pick up the slack. We worked as a team and fed off each other artistically. Sadly, my mother passed away peacefully in her sleep while attending a quilt show in 1997. The first edition of this book was at press, and she did not get to see a finished copy. Nor did she get to see what a stir the book would cause among manufacturers who serviced the quilting industry, helping them improve their products in order to help quilters improve their hand stitching.

Over the last ten years, I have watched the quilting industry evolve. My daughter Victoria began quilting at age eight, and won her first gold ribbon at age nine. She began teaching her own classes on a national level at age 15. I can't tell you the pride I feel in being part of a three-generation quilting family. It has been fun to watch the trends come and go—as a judge at major quilting shows, I get to see them all. It is even more interesting to see how the tools and products we use in the age-old craft of hand-quilting change from year to year.

All quilters are, or should be, concerned about the quality of their work. But quality is particularly important for hand quilters. The beauty of a handmade quilt is that, when done well, it endures to become an heirloom that is passed down through generations. Longevity, however, does not result from the skill of the quilter alone. Every product used in making the quilt—from the fabric and the batting to the needle, thread, and other supplies—contributes to the quality of the workmanship. Just as important, every technique the quilter uses affects the beauty and the life span of the quilt.

Mom used to say that we inherited our quilting genes from my great grandmother, Gladys Lee. I believe we inherited something else, too. That is the ability to break down a complicated task into its component parts so that others can learn a technique more easily. For a quilting teacher, that talent is even more valuable than the gift of quilting. It is through our teaching that my mother and I are able to convey our passion to others.

If you, too, are passionate about quilting, this book will be your ultimate reference for selecting materials and supplies that will make your quilting experience more pleasurable and more successful. Every quilt we make has a different purpose or master plan. The information, charts, and product comparisons in this book will help you make educated choices for each quilt, minimizing wasted time, effort, or money spent. Even more important, this book shares orthopaedically correct techniques that will help you extend your quilting lifetime without casing you pain or joint damage. It is my hope that this book also becomes an inspiration for all you who whish to improve your stitches and make more beautiful, longer-lasting quilts. Enjoy and create!

Dierdra A. McElroy

CHAPTER ONE

Fabrics

When you look at antique quilts, you will see that almost all are made from cotton fabrics. There is a simple reason—in the early days of quilting, fabrics of any other fiber were extremely rare. Even today, when many other choices are available, those who make traditional quilts usually choose cotton in order to replicate the designs of the past. We have an enormous amount of freedom in the fabrics we choose, yet not all choices are conducive to achieving That Perfect Stitch. Some fabrics are simply more difficult to quilt than others, making tiny, even stitches impossible, no matter how expert the quilter. Once you understand the differences between fabrics and the ways in which they are made, you are better able to predict the effect on your stitch.

Dash It All. Made by Bettina Havig. *This traditional quilt design is hand pieced and hand quilted. Collection of Dierdra A. McElroy*

Warp and Weft

Yarns are threads woven to make fabrics. Yarns that run parallel to the selvages are the warp of the fabric; yarns that run across from selvage to selvage are the weft. It is easy—just remember "weft is left!"

Fabrics Suited to Quilting

It can take up to a thousand hours to make a quilt by hand. When we begin, we all have high hopes that the quilt we make will become a family heirloom and will pass down through generations. Yet no matter how beautiful the quilt or how carefully it is sewn, if it is not made from the right fabrics, it is not going to stand the test of time.

We know from seeing antique quilts that certain fabrics are more fragile than others and deteriorate more quickly. Silks, velvets, and satins, popular in antique crazy quilts, have rotted away in quilts that were frequently used or poorly cared for. Fabrics like these, because of their weave and texture, are impossible to hand quilt well. Crazy quilts, after all, were tied rather than quilted. The same is true of flannel and wool fabrics. Although wool stands up to years of wear, the loose weave makes it unsuitable for fine hand quilting. The fibers in flannel are weak and, once the "fluff" of the individual yarns is worn away, the fabric is very sparse. Heavy fabrics like denim, corduroy, and double knits are equally inappropriate for hand quilting. Also, avoid any fabric that stretches excessively when pulled on the straight of the grain. These fabrics are too unstable; the quilting process draws the fabric in the direction you are quilting, and you will most likely have a rippled quilt when you are finished.

Understanding Fabric Construction

The fabrics we choose have to meet other requirements besides the ability to stand the test of time. Most important, the *weave* of the fabric can have a dramatic affect on your ability to achieve smaller, more even stitches that will show nicely on the surface of your quilt. If the weave is too tight, quilting is physically challenging. If you suffer from carpel tunnel syndrome or arthritis or have other hand challenges, quilting through a tight weave is an almost impossible task. Some fabrics are woven too loosely for fine hand quilting and will not allow you to get the smaller stitches you seek. Most contemporary fabrics on the market are a mixture of both too tight *and* too loose. How can this be possible?

Fabric is woven in two directions. As it winds off the bolt, the grain lines that runs up and down is called the *warp* (see blue arrow in diagram). The grain line that runs selvage to selvage across the fabric is known as the *weft* (see red arrow). The diagonal to the weft and warp is called the *bias* (see green arrow). When you pull on the fabric, the bias should feel stretchy. There is not supposed to be much stretch along the weft or the warp.

For quality fabric suited to hand quilting or hand appliqué the weave should be as even as possible. To determine whether a piece of fabric is woven evenly, all you need to do is to count the number of yarns (threads) woven in a one inch increment in each grain line. Evenly woven fabrics have the same number of yarns per inch in the warp and in the weft. You'll find that the *thread count* of most fabrics are not absolutely even; a common ratio in today's fabric is 68/56, that is 68 yarns to the inch (27 yarns to the cm) in the warp and 56 yarns to the inch (22 yarns to the cm) in the weft. This means that in most commercial fabrics there are 12 more yarns per inch running to the warp than there are to the weft (5 more yarns per cm). I have found that if the thread count varies by more than six to eight yarns per inch, the fabric is not suited to hand quilting or appliqué and can have detrimental effects on your project. The uneven balance of powers in the weave causes the fabric to stretch dramatically more in one grain line than the other. This can cause your hand stitches to vary in size, depending on the direction you are quilting with the grain line.

Unevenly woven fabrics do not stretch equally in each direction and they tend to fray. The more uneven the thread count, the worse the fraying. The bias is dramatically more stretchy than in evenly woven fabrics, making it extremely difficult to obtain a completely flat and square finished project. Quality fabrics with even thread counts make quilting, sewing, piecing, and appliqué a pleasure to do, while lesser quality fabrics make the process less enjoyable. Worse still, the finished project does not highlight your true abilities as a quilter.

Learning to look for evenly woven fabrics will not only make your projects more fun, but will allow you to achieve better workmanship with less effort. The result is a quilt that should last many more years, even generations. You might start off thinking that you are making a quilt you intend to be used, abused, and loved by grandchildren, so quality shouldn't matter. I wholeheartedly agree that this is the best and most time-honored reason to make a quilt. But remember that those precious grandchildren will be able to drag around the special quilt grandma made for a few years more if it is made from quality fabrics and quilted more densely with smaller stitches!

Finding Quality Fabrics

Feeling for stretch is a quick and easy method you can use to check thread count when shopping for fabrics. While researching thread count,

Know Your Fabric

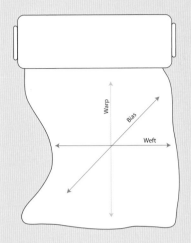

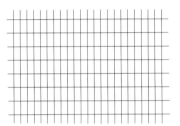

Unevenly woven fabric

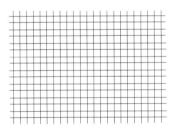

Evenly woven fabric

I developed a tool that allows for a much more accurate measure: the Roxanne Optimal Strand Estimator, or the ROSE, described on the next page. This inexpensive tool combines the benefits of a magnifying lens and a ruler into a simple plastic strip. It slips easily into your purse for shopping trips. Keep one in your sewing room, too, so that you can double-check fabrics in your stash before you commit to sewing them into a quilt. The ROSE may be the answer you are looking for if you have any problems with excessive fraying, uneven stretch or uneven shrinkage. Once you improve the quality of the fabrics you use, you will quickly find you have less trouble with hand-appliquéd points or curves, precision piecing, and uneven quilting stitches.

Quality fabrics with even thread counts cost more to manufacture than most commercial fabrics. That is why I always recommend purchasing your fabrics from quality quilt shops, rather than from non-specialist sewing shops or discount stores. However, while even-thread count fabrics may cost more, the difference they make to your sewing is amazing. You will immediately notice that good fabrics make piecing, appliqué, and quilting much more fun! The needle glides through easily, resulting in nice, even stitches, with less stress on your fingers. You'll get better workmanship with less effort. Sewn pieces have little or no stretch, and minimal fraying. Best of all, with quality fabrics your quilted projects will last many more years than those made with inferior fabrics.

Mixing Fibers

If a quilter were to make two identical quilts, one of polyester-blend fabrics and one of 100 percent cotton, they would have an identical appraised value. The only thing that would reduce the value would be if the quilter mixed the two fibers within the same quilt. Polyester is stronger than cotton and so even a tiny patch of polyester in a cotton quilt will damage the quilt over time, or vice versa. For longevity, a balance of powers is needed.

For Tucker. Made by Margaret Illions, Las Vegas, NV.
Butterflies in appliqué and channel appliqué. The quilting is done in large concentric circles.

ROSE: A Tool for Checking Thread Counts

Before developing the Roxanne Optimal Strand Estimator, I would always carry a magnifying lens and a ruler with me when shopping for fabric. I would pull them out and fumble over the fabric, trying to do a quick thread count before purchasing. The ROSE is a wonderful little tool that helps you measure thread counts quickly and easily. Here is how to use it.

1. Remove the ROSE from its protective sleeve. Make sure it is right side up and you can read "ROSE" at the top.

2. Place the fabric flat on a hard surface. Position the ROSE diagonally over the fabric as shown.

3. Relax your eyes and then look at the tool as it lies on the fabric. Resist the urge to focus on the fabric by looking through the "window" of the ROSE.

4. *Slowly rotate* the ROSE clockwise. You will begin to see a "rainbow" of faint warping lines across the middle of the tool.

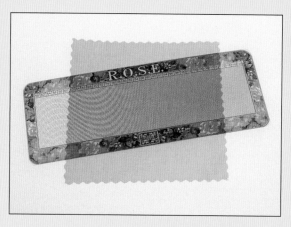

5. Continue rotating and notice that the "rainbow" becomes more sharply arched. Just before the tool becomes horizontal, those arched lines will be at their peak. Be sure to keep the ROSE flat and smooth on your fabric.

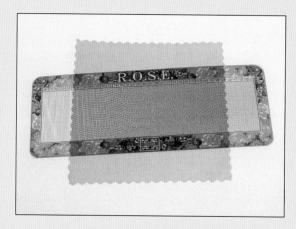

This arched image is called a *moiré* pattern. It occurs due to the way your eyes communicate with your brain when sets of parallel lines overlap in a slightly uneven way. In this case, the ROSE tool has one set of parallel lines while the grain of fabric has another set of lines. Each person may see the moiré pattern slightly differently, based on the way the brain listens to the eyes

6. Follow the middle or peak of the arch up to the number bar across the top of the ROSE. In this sample, the peak of the arch rests at 82, so the thread count of the warp is 82 yarns to the inch.

7. Return to the beginning position in step 2. This time, rotate the ROSE the other way, stopping when it is almost vertical on the fabric.

8. Follow the peak of the arch to the number bar across the top of the ROSE. This will show you the number of yarns to the inch in the weft of the fabric. If the difference between the two numbers is more than 8, seriously reconsider before buying the fabric. If both numbers are above 75 and the difference between them is 8 or less, then you have found a quality quilting fabric.

Helpful Hints

* ROSE is accurate to plus or minus one yarn per inch

* Make sure you have a good light source and angle of vision. Daylight and artificial light are equally adequate, but reflections may interfere with the moiré effect. Experiment with light sources and angles of vision to determine optimal conditions for your eyes.

* On fabrics with strong prints, try using the ROSE on the reverse side, where the patterns are less visible.

* Experiment with fabrics in your stash until you are comfortable seeing the moiré pattern. If you have trouble seeing it when the ROSE is horizontal, rotate both fabric and tool to the vertical position and try again.

* If the moiré pattern peaks downwards rather than up into the number bar, slowly rotate the tool counterclockwise until the moiré shifts position.

* Do not leave your ROSE unprotected, as it may "wilt" if left in direct sunlight or other sources of heat. Store it in its protective sleeve to avoid scratches. Mild scratches will not interfere with its effectiveness, but rough handling will. Never fold your ROSE. To clean, use a soft cloth and any cleanser you would use on eyewear.

The ROSE was developed by Roxanne Products International and is now available from Colonial Needle Co. (www.colonialneedle.com)

Finding That Perfect Weave

The fabrics we choose have to meet other requirements, besides the ability to stand the test of time. First, the weave must be right. The ideal fabric for hand quilting is one that is woven at about to 75 to 86 threads per inch (30 to 34 threads per cm) in *each direction*. If the weave is too tight, it makes quilting an almost impossible task. Pima cotton is woven 132 yarns per inch (52 yarns per cm) to the weft and 100 yarns per inch (40 yarns per cm) to the warp! Bedsheets are generally made from pima cotton and that is the main reason why you should never use a bedsheet to back a quilt. Note, too, that batik designs are usually done on pima cottons.

The weave of some fabrics is too loose to quilt well, especially if your stitches are small. The smaller your stitches become, there will be a time when you see that they are so small that the needle can actually rise and descend through the fabric without catching a single yarn of the quilt top or backing. This means you are simply too good for that particular fabric! Any fabric that is woven less than 60 yarns per inch (24 yarns per cm) to the warp and 60 yarns per inch (24 yarns per cm) to the weft will produce this effect for better quilters.

To compound this problem, fabrics with a loose weave are usually heavier than others, meaning that each yarn is fatter in diameter. After having carefully observed several hundred quilting stitches under a microscope, I have determined that quilting will never split the yarn of a fabric. In every single case, the yarn rolls in one direction or the other and forces the point of the needle through the intersections between yarns. This means that if the yarn is too fat, the needle simply will not go where you want it to, resulting in uneven stitches.

Grades of Fabric

Manufacturers rarely produce fabrics specifically for quilting. Most fabrics are meant for the clothing or decorator industry. In the last 20 years, the quilting industry has grown large enough to attract the attention of manufacturers and many of them advertise directly for this target market. Even so, many of the fabrics that find their way into quilt shops or craft stores do not meet the thread count requirements for quality quilts. Since thread counts are not listed on the ends of bolts, there is little guidance given to help quilters make their selections. It is up to you to train your eye to look past the gorgeous prints and colors. You need to pay attention to fabric construction and decide whether the weave is too loose or too tight for your purposes.

Mermaids in the Surf. Made by Roxanne McElroy.

Echo-quilted with simple outline quilting around appliqué of waves. Can you tell which of the background fabrics was not prewashed?

Not only do manufacturers make different fabrics for different purposes, they also create more than one grade of each fabric type. Second-grade fabrics are less expensive, and for very good reasons. Some are not only low in thread count, but the individual yarns from which they are made are thinner, making the weave very loose and resulting in a lightweight fabric. On top of that, the thread count is often inconsistent across the fabric. Some leading manufacturers print identical designs on first- and second-grade fabrics, and market them under different brand names to different retail stores, chains, or discount wholesalers. Don't always rely on brand name as an assurance of quality. To be sure, pull out your trusty ROSE thread counter to check!

You can sometimes find wonderful fabrics at discount prices—all that is wrong with them is that the colors did not print quite right. Some fabrics have as many as 17 colors and each one must be stamped separately onto the fabric. If even one of those colors is slightly out of place or is missing altogether, the fabric is discarded by the manufacturer and sold only as a second-grade fabric to discount stores, if sold at all. The consumer will not be able to tell there is a color problem. As a general rule of thumb, before you buy any discounted fabric, first check the thread count. If it looks good and you like the design, buy it.

The Mathematics of It All

A quilter intentionally sets out to quilt 10 stitches per inch (4 stitches per cm). Her fabric is a 60/60 (24/24) thread count. Divide 60 by 10 to make 6 (divide 24 by 4 to make 6). She must use 6 threads to complete each individual stitch, which means 3 threads must pass over the needle and 3 threads must pass under the needle. You can see that trying to quilt any more than 10 stitches per inch (4 stitches per cm) on this fabric would be impossible. The quilter would be weaving, not stitching! Likewise once you understand the mathematics it becomes plain that fabrics with uneven thread counts can cause uneven quilting stitches. A quilter may be quilting 14 stitches per inch (5.5 stitches per cm) traveling to the weft on a 78/56 (30/22) thread count fabric, but as soon as she changes directions (which is inevitable) she is relegated to less than 10 per inch (4 stitches per cm), no matter how hard she may try.

Bird Flees the Thorns. Made by Joe Cunningham, San Francisco, CA.
Machine pieced, hand appliqued and hand quilted.

Quilting Painted Fabrics

Painted fabrics are more difficult to quilt than other fabrics because the paint is a foreign substance that has to be penetrated by the needle before it can get through the fiber itself. The heavier the paint, the harder the quilt job. Paint on fabric has, in the past, yellowed with age. Heavily painted fabrics can even crack and peel. Remember, paint is a surface application only. Lightly painted fabrics can be washed off in several washings or wear off with time. Beautiful gold and silver accent prints are no exception. I am personally drawn to these fabrics for their stunning beauty. I use them and love them, knowing full well the paint will be gone by the time my grandchild inherits. Remember, one secret to enjoying quilting is not compromising your choices to a point that it makes quilting a chore—enjoy painted fabrics while they last!

Should Quilters Prewash Fabrics?

I prewash all my fabrics, but I have come across many quilters who are reluctant to do so. Some prefer not to prewash because they like the feel of the fiber with the original sizing still in it. (Sizing is the process through which manufacturers press a finishing coat onto a fabric to give it extra body.) There is a simple remedy for this, however—using spray sizing when the fabric is pressed will replenish the original look and feel. Other quilters think that the fabric somehow changes in the washing process. In fact, there are only a very few fabrics that "change." Examples include chintz, sateen, and polished cottons. Since the unique sheen on these fabrics is a surface treatment done through a heat-pressing process, the sheen naturally goes away with washing. These fabrics are exciting and add an interesting look to a new quilt. I have made quilts using them, knowing full well that the sheen would disappear. Sometimes, I just cannot resist these fabrics and feel that, however temporary, that lovely effect is worth the effort while it lasts.

There are a couple of overwhelming arguments in favor of prewashing your fabrics. First, fabric tends to shrink. In the manufacturing process, fabrics are woven to a standard 48" (120 cm) wide, selvage to selvage. During the dyeing and printing process a print cloth will usually shrink by about 3" (8 cm). When the fabric reaches your quilt shop it is usually about 44" to 45" (110 cm to 115 cm) wide, as indicated on the ends of the bolts. Crossover fabrics shrink a little more due to their weight and the thickness of the yarn, coming into the shops at about 43″ (109 cm) wide. The yarns found in homespun fabrics are of a nature that they shrink drastically, sometimes to less than 41″ (104 cm) wide! Simple logic tells us that a quilt made with dozens or even hundreds of different fabrics that were not prewashed will become severely puckered with its first washing. In time, the fabrics that do not shrink much will put excess stress on the ones that shrink drastically, tearing them out of the quilt.

The second argument for always prewashing your fabrics revolves around the dyes that are used. No matter what a manufacturer says, fabric dyes are still unstable. Some are worse than others, obviously, but there is no way to tell by just looking at a fabric which ones will cause trouble. The traditional method of prewashing fabrics in solutions of salt or vinegar rarely helps set the colors. There is a product on the market called Retayne that has received good reviews and does a little better. For best results, follow the directions on the bottle carefully, making sure the water is the correct temperature. Never trust that fabrics will be colorfast—there are few things in quilting more devastating than seeing colors bleed into surrounding fabrics.

I wash all my fabrics in a regular machine-wash cycle and dry them on a regular setting, too. I am not gentle and do not believe in using the gentle cycle for quilting fabrics. I check the water in the final rinse by removing some of it in a clear glass cup. If the water has any tint at all, the fabric gets washed again. I do this three times and then, if the fabric is still throwing off dyes, I do not use it in my quilt and neither should you. It is as simple as that.

There are quilters out their that say their quilts will simply never be washed. It is true, you could put a label on the back of your quilt saying "Over my dead body wash this quilt!" That is exactly what will happen. One of your family members will feel compelled to wash the quilt no matter what your wishes might have been. It happens all the time!

Ironing Fabric

It has been my observation that quilters tend to iron their fabrics far too much. While most quilters worry about washing fabrics, they do not seem to realize the damage that is done by excessive ironing. Irons can heat to more than 360°F (182°C), which is hot enough to scorch cotton. This is akin to the techniques used to obtain polished cottons. Iron your fabric only as much as needed to take out creases. Avoid resting the iron in any one particular spot. Pressing the iron down in

Annette's Bavarian Scrolls. Designed by Helen Squire, quilted by Dierdra A. McElroy.
This pretty round piece showcases a quilting design of crosshatching and ornate curliques.

one place allows a build-up of extreme heat that has no escape and severely damages the yarns of the fabric. A good example would be to look at a pair of jeans that you iron regularly. Look at where you usually iron in the creases, and you will notice that the color is faded. This is a sign of damaged fibers caused from extreme heat build-up on the fold.

Quilter's Workshop

1. Piece together 20 5″ × 5″ (12 cm × 12 cm) squares of different fabric brands. Mark the brand name on each square with a permanent pen. Using a good polyester batting and a muslin backing, sandwich and baste the practice quilt together. With a waxed quilting thread in a color that is easily visible and your favorite brand of needle in a size 10, quilt a simple design on each block. On the back of your sampler mark your impressions on the ease of quilting. You might even want to get a magnifying lens or use the ROSE tool (see page 14) and take note of the thread count.

2. Pull a couple of ½ yard (0.5m) pieces of red fabric from your stash and wash them along with a piece of pure white cotton fabric. At the last rinse cycle, stop the machine and dip a clear cup into the tub for a sample of water. Evaluate for clarity. When the cycle is complete, remove the fabrics and inspect them. Did the white fabric absorb any red dye? Repeat this experiment with different red fabrics, making note of brand names, if possible.

CHAPTER TWO

Batting

From old blankets to horsehair, all kinds of materials have been used to stuff quilts. Some of our ancestors were lucky and could use cotton, picked from nearby fields. Other quilters, however, were desperate enough to use horsehair or even dog hair. One recently discovered antique quilt was batted with newspaper! A rather unusual quilt in Hawaii even had tobacco leaves for batting. We are fortunate today to have a multitude of batting choices, each with a different feel and look. We can choose from cotton, polyester, cotton-polyester blend, wool, silks, bamboo, and even alpaca. Some battings are easier to quilt than others, and each gives a quilt a different finished look and feel. Most quilters pick different battings for almost every quilt they make.

Gingko. Made by Roxanne McElroy.
Notice how the basting stitches radiate from the center. The quilt top is based on a Japanese family crest design that is more than a thousand years old. The quilt is photographed in the Grace Frame.

Kang Kang Sul Le.
Made by Yong Ho Halt.
*With wide stippling on the
mountain and bushes, the
quilting design follows the
fabric pattern itself. The quilter
used fabric paints for highlights
and shadows for the pagoda.*

Batting Fibers

Cotton

The time-honored batting is, of course, cotton. Cotton is a natural fiber and generally produces a soft and cuddly quilt. Cotton is a good choice, because it is time proven and it does not *beard*—a phenomenon where batting fibers poke up through fabrics in a finished quilt. Other battings simply have not been around long enough to know how they will wear over time. I suspect that many batts flatten or break up into clumps, given enough time.

If it is important to you to use a natural fiber in your batting you are limited to cotton, wool, silk or bamboo. One appeal of cotton is that it is cooler to sleep under than the other choices. It is also less expensive and more easily found. The biggest issue with today's cotton batts is that they do not needle as well as polyester, and so the quilting stitches are not quite perfect. Your hands have to work much harder to push a needle through cotton batting, so I generally do not recommend quilters to use it if they have "hand-challenges," such as arthritis, carpel tunnel syndrome, or tendonitis. In order for any cotton batt to be remotely suited to hand quilting, it has to be very thin (low loft). For this reason, if I use a cotton batting, I have to consider it as one compromise in my quilt. You can expect cotton battings to shrink by anywhere from two percent to eight percent. Some are designed to shrink a little more for that "antique puckered" look, which is nice if that is what you want.

Another problem with cotton is that some brands have not rid their product of cotton seed sloughs. Quilting into these can cause finger joint pain as well as uneven quilting stitches as the quilter is forced to go around the seed. It is not unheard of for the oils that these seeds contain to migrate out into the quilt top, staining it permanently. The thinner a cotton batting is made, the more quiltable it will be. Terms such as "needle punched" or "resin bonded" tend to be tell-tale clues that the batting will not be much fun to work with by hand.

Some quilters like to limit the amount of quilting and spread their stitching more than up to 5" (13 cm) apart. If you are using cotton batting, you need to quilt more densely than this, despite manufacturers' recommendations. I personally quilt every 1" (2.4 cm) to ensure that the layers meld into a single unit.

Polyester

Polyester battings are the most prevalent and least costly choice. They are available in a variety of thicknesses and are frequently blended with other types of fibers. Each gives a quilt a different look and feel. Thinner battings are definitely the easiest to hand quilt, since they require less pressure to push the needle through the batting. They are also generally less expensive to buy than other battings. Mixing a polyester batting into a cotton quilt will not, according to quilt appraisers, devalue your quilt in any way. What the polyester does for you is provide a much more "slippery pathway" than cotton for your needle to glide through. I always look for a polyester batting that appears to have an even

Batting Brands

Brand	Fiber	Cost	Ease	Loft	Main Features	Effect on Stitch
Hobb's Washable	Wool	$$$$	9	L	Take care to select fabrics with good thread counts and quilt closely to avoid bearding. Can be washed, but should be air dried. Makes for a warm quilt to sleep under.	Produces fine quilting stitches.
Warm & Natural Wool	Wool	$$$	9	L	Same as above. 3% to 5% shrinkage.	Needles well and produces nice stitches.
Fairfield Wool	Wool	$$$	9	M	Same as above	Needles well, slightly thicker loft for more relief in finished quilt.
Bamboo Batting	50% Bamboo 50% Cotton	$$$	2	M	2% to 3% shrinkage. Some acti-bacterial properties and mildew resistant but needs to be protected from moths.	Unsuited to hand quilting.
Silk	Silk	$$$$	10	M-H	Needles like a hot knife through butter, launders beautifully, breathes, and has a gorgeous drape. Difficult to find and costly.	If I could afford it, I would use no other!
Hobbs Silk	90% Silk 10% Polyester	$$$$	6	M	Although mostly silk, the bonding process prevents warping around tip of needle.	Less expensive than pure silk, but your hands have to work harder for less perfect stitches.
Eco-Craft by Mountain Mist	100% PLA	$$	4	L	A manmade natural fiber batting derived from plants and fully biodegradable. There is some debate as to whether it is truly eco-friendly because it turns a food crop, corn, into batting.	Very difficult to needle by hand, producing large, uneven stitches and sore fingers.
Mountain Mist Blue Ribbon	Cotton	$	6	L	3% to 5% shrinkage, making it ideal for creating an antique, puckered look. Does not prewash well.	Needles nicely for a cotton batting, producing beautiful quilts.
Hobb's Heirloom	80% Cotton 20% Polyester	$$	5	L	Same as above	Same as above.
Hobb's Organic	Cotton	$$	4	L	For hand quilting, make sure you get the batting *without scrim*—a fine netting attached to one side to act as a stabilizer for machine quilting.	Satisfactory.

Brand	Fiber	Cost	Ease	Loft	Main Features	Effect on Stitch
Warm & Natural	Cotton	$$	2	L	This batting is coarse and stiff and has many slubs that get in the way of the needle. Pre-washing does not help. Seed oils from the slubs can stain the quilt after it is finished. 3-5% shrinkage.	Causes stitches to look uneven, as quilter dodges slubs. Unsuitable for hand quilting.
Quilter's Cotton	Cotton	$$	6	L	Also coarse and stiff. It takes a tremendous amount of pressure to force the needle through this batting, making the fingers sore very quickly.	Difficult to achieve small stitches without pain. Unsuitable for hand quilting.
Fairfield Soft Touch	Cotton	$$$	6	L	A pristine white batting that is very smooth and evenly pressed. No prewashing is necessary.	A good option if you must use cotton, Extremely low loft, producing very little relief in the quilt.
Fairfield Cotton Classic	80% Cotton 20% Polyester	$$$	8	L	As the factory sprays a thin silicon coating on the batting to make it easier to package, it requires special treatment before use. This coating will not hurt a quilt, it only makes it harder to needle. Unroll and soak the batt in cool water for a few minutes. Hand wring and put in the dryer on a polyester setting. It may take a couple of cycles to dry. Once treated, this batting makes a soft, cuddly quilt any child—or adult—would love.	Needles well, once washed.
Mountain Mist Rose	Cotton	$$	8	L	A beautiful white batting that is evenly lofted and soft to the touch. No need to prewash, and only 1% to 2% shrinkage. Available in bleached white or natural.	The best choice among cotton battings for small, even stitches, due to thin loft. I was able to achieve 14 stitches per inch, with only a little stress.
Hobbs Cloud Loft 'Fat Batt'	Polyester	$$$	2	H	Designed for tied, comforter style quilts. The loft is too high to hand quilt well.	Produces large, uneven stitches. Unsuitable for hand quilting.
Fairfield Hi Loft	Polyester	$	2	H	Same as above	Same as above.
Fairfield Extra Loft	Polyester	$	7	M	A unique batting that squishes down to make very fine quilting stitches and then puffs up in between stitched lines to give the quilt a comforter look.	Quilts nicely. Avoid quilting too closely, or the special features of the high loft are defeated.

Brand	Fiber	Cost	Ease	Loft	Main Features	Effect on Stitch
Mountain Mist Quilt	Polyester	$	10	L	This is a medium to low loft batt that is very even. It consistently unrolls out of the bag easily without folds or kinks.	A great all-purpose, light inexpensive batt that will produce tiny, even hand stitches.
Hobb's Thermore	Polyester	$	10	XL	Originally made for wearable arts, this batt has virtually no loft. It is very evenly woven and makes lightweight quilts.	Produces small, even stitches, but little relief.
Fairfield Low Loft	Polyester	$	10	XL	This batting is even thinner than Hobb's Thermore, but it does have some loft. Sometimes we compromise a quilt with an extra heavy fabric. Using an extra-thin batting can often reverse the compromise.	Though it needles well. this batting seems too thin for quilting, as a finished quilt can feel like it lacks any stuffing at all.
Mountain Mist Mini Light	Polyester	$	10	XL	An extremely low-loft batting For lightweight quilts or wearable arts.	Produces small even stitches, but little relief.
Heritage Collection: A Touch of Silk	95% Polyester 5% Silk	$	10	M	A consistently evenly lofted batting that is slightly thicker in loft. The small amount of silk carded in makes this batting needle beautifully	My favorite for all-purpose hand quilting and for all my student kits
Fairfield Traditional	Polyester	$	7	L	A good choice for a quilt that is heavy but not thick. It is reminiscent of years gone by when quilters used old flannel blankets as batting.	Produces a heavy quilt with fine stitches.
Hobb's Poly-Down	Polyester	$	6	L	This batting is uneven in its overall density, which is readily seen when held up to a light.	Causes uneven stitches stitches as the quilter passes through denser denser and thinner areas.
Hobb's Black Batt	Polyester	$	6	L	A black version of Hobb's Poly-Down, designed for overall darker quilts. The black batt makes fibers that migrate to the surface less visible. Be sure to test lighter fabrics against the batt before committing it to the quilt.	Same as above.

Based on my personal examinations of products I have used

thickness throughout. This is easy to see when you hold the batting up to a light. Blending polyester into other fibers, such as cotton, makes the cotton more quiltable, yet you can look at this another way: the cotton content makes the polyester harder to quilt. I recommend looking at the percentages of cotton versus polyester to determine quiltability.

Wool

Wool battings have been used for generations and are especially popular in colder climates. Wool batting is the warmest batt you can use, which is good if you live in North Dakota, but not if you live in San Diego! Most wool battings launder as well as polyester batts, and I have always found them to be very smooth and easy to quilt. Do not dry wool batts in a dryer because wool felts under heat. Air dry wool batts instead. The major flaw with woolen batts, however, is that they tend to beard; the batting fibers work their way up through the quilt top. Bearding can be heart-wrenching—the quilt looks as though a Persian cat took a nap on it, but whenever you pull the hairs off they are replaced by more! No one knows for sure what causes bearding, but my research has shown that eight out of ten times a wool batting was used, often in conjunction with a loose weave fabric. The spacing of the quilting may also have something to do with it, since I have never seen a heavily quilted quilt—with quilting lines no more than 1″ (2.5 cm) apart—beard.

Silk

The most exotic batting, though it has become increasingly hard to find, is 100 percent silk. It must be unrolled carefully onto the quilt back and smoothed and fussed with a little more than other battings. Silk batting has a "clingy" quality that is a real advantage because it does not shift around between the layers of the quilt while you stitch. To quote one fellow quilter, "It quilts just like a hot knife through butter." It produces fine, even stitches with great ease on the hand. The silk batting I have used in the past is made from mulberry trees grown in China, and it launders the same as polyester in both the washer and dryer. Pure silk battings have the ability to wick moisture out of the surrounding air, making quilts warm in the winter time and cool in the summer time. In recent years, pure silk battings have all but disappeared off the market in favor of silk blends. Hobbs Bonded Fibers has a 90% silk/10% polyester batting. Known as Tuscany Silk, it is resin bonded, which makes the silk batt much easier to lay out onto a quilt. However, the bonding process has also made the batting no fun to hand quilt. Mountain Mist has a

Black Batts

Not all batting is white. Battings range from pure snowy white to ecru to black! Hobb's Black Batt was designed to use in Amish quilts where the majority of the fabrics are dark. The idea was to limit the effects of bearding by making escaped fibers less noticeable. Using black batting also helps maintain the integrity of the colors, since sometimes white behind blacks and dark blues makes them look a little faded or washed out. If you are making an Amish quilt and plan to use black batt, it might be a good idea to take your quilt top into the store and lay the lightest fabric in it over the package of black batt. Occasionally the batt will shadow through lighter colors, defeating the purpose of the batt. Doing this ahead of time could avoid disappointments.

Wedding Rings and Champagne Bubbles on a Bed of Roses. Made by Roxanne McElroy.

The appliqué design is quite simple. It is the quilting design that makes this quilt special. There are petals and leaves within the design, thorns too—a reminder that marriage is not always a bed of roses. The quilting pattern is shown on pages 162 to 163.

new batting line called Heritage Collection, which includes a batting called A Touch of Silk. This batt is 95% polyester/5% silk. The tiny amount of silk makes it a highly quiltable batting for practically a polyester cost! A quilt made with silk batting is warmer than a cotton or polyester quilt but not as warm as a wool quilt. The only disadvantage to silk batting, besides the extra effort in laying it out, is the cost. Also, it is very hard to find. I have been unable to find a good source. Still, silk batting will give you the most sensual quilt you'll ever make!

Bamboo

Anyone that has seen bamboo has a difficult time imagining that it can be used to make a soft, cuddly batting for a quilt, yet it has emerged as an environmentally conscious alternative for quilts. Bamboo has natural

antibacterial properties, is mildew resistant, and, as a natural fiber, it is breathable. Most bamboo battings are blended with organic cotton and, although soft to the touch, are not easy to push a needle through for fine hand quilting stitches. Bamboo is a fairly new fiber to our industry, leaving some doubt as to its long term effects inside quilts. Already, quilters have noticed some issues with the batting "yellowing" and showing through white fabrics. Many reviews state that bamboo batting "feels like silk". It is definitely softer than most pure cotton battings but does not approach the luxury of a pure silk batting. Bamboo battings shrink by two to three inches if they are cotton blended and they tend to be very densely needle-punched.

Alpaca

Alpaca is a luxurious wool which is hypoallergenic so it doesn't cause the same allergic reactions that other wools might. Alpacas grow hair instead of fur, so 100 percent alpaca has a propensity to beard, as the longer, thinner wool hairs find their way up through loose weave fabrics very easily. If you quilt densely, bearding can be avoided. Because of bearding, many companies blend cotton or other wools into the alpaca to stabilize it, but this can make the batting more difficult to stitch through. A quilt made with alpaca batting must be laundered carefully and never dried in a heated dryer. Alpacas are amazing animals and their hair is the only known natural fiber that is 100 percent naturally flame retardant. It also does not get that "wet wool" smell during laundering. Most companies offering Alpaca battings are working with rescue groups that are actively involved in rescue and rehabilitation efforts of these Camelids from South America. The animal is only sheered once every two years, limiting the availability of the fiber and thus increasing its cost. I made a quilt with 100 percent Alpaca purchased from Inca Fashions in Fresno, California, and it quilted as nicely as silk!

Batting Loft

The *loft* of a quilt describes the degree to which the quilt puffs up around the quilting stitches. The loft of the batting you choose is really a matter of personal taste. In years past, high-loft battings have been popular, while more recently the trend has been toward a thinner look. There are no rules regarding which batting is appropriate for a specific type of quilt. You may want to consider the ease of quilting—higher loft battings are a little harder to hand quilt. Take into consideration, too, the purpose of the quilt. If it is a wall hanging, a lower loft lies flatter against the wall and creates smaller dust-collecting ledges!

Preparing Batting for Quilting

Whichever batting you select, it is always a good idea to open the package and unroll the batting. Allow it to lie flat on a bed, table, or floor for 24 hours before sandwiching it in a quilt. This allows the crinkles to settle and smooth out. The batting should be about 4″ (10 cm) wider and 4″ (10 cm) longer than the quilt top. It can be cut to fit later. If the batting is too small, two pieces can be joined by butting them up together and sewing with large overcast stitches. Do not allow overlapping, however minor.

Some quilters feel the need to prewash their batting. In my experience, most battings don't weather prewashing well. At best, they stretch unevenly, leaving high/low spots which will cause uneven stitches later on. At worst, they practically disintegrate in the washer, resulting in clumps of batting. Of course, this can have a dramatic effect on your stitches, not to mention the extra time wasted. Battings should be ready to go straight out of the bag. Prewashing cotton batts can prevent shrinkage within the finished quilt, but if you aren't looking for that old-fashioned, crinkly look then don't use a cotton batting. Or at least, don't select one with a high shrinkage rate.

How Closely Should I Quilt?

Amazingly enough, the batting companies give recommendations on how far apart you can quilt with their batts. Several say "up to 8 inches" (up to 20 cm), which means you can leave the width of this page unquilted! As a quilt judge at national shows, I always encourage my students to add more quilting. I strongly recommend never leaving more than 3″ (7.5 cm) unquilted. This is both for design aesthetics, as well as, to ensure the longevity of the quilt. If it a quilt that will be used and loved. Quilt even more densely. I rarely leave much more than a square inch unquilted in my quilts.

Quilter's Workshop

Select as many batts as possible and cut them into small squares. Join them together by using overcast stitches. Sandwich the pieced batting with muslin and mark each batting name on the quilt backing. Using simple templates, trace a design on the muslin over each different batting. Quilt each with the same size and type of needle and the same brand of thread. Compare the results and write them in permanent ink in each square on the back of the quilt.

Needles

Most of us take needles for granted. All we consider when we choose one from a new pack is the size of the eye, and, after that, we barely think twice about it. The only time we get out a new needle is if we lose or break the first one. Considering that needles are the key tool in hand quilting, we really should think carefully about the choices we make and the ways in which we use them. For it is only when you use the needle that is perfect for the quilt you are making that you will be able to achieve That Perfect Stitch. All needles wear and dull with use, and that use should not exceed 8 to 10 hours per needle. Look for the best-quality needle at a price at which you will feel no guilt about throwing it away for a fresh one.

Hibiscus Quilt. Made by Margaret Illions, Las Vegas, NV.
This large scale design features perfect straight-line and curve-line quilting.

How the Very Best Needles Are Made

Needle making started as a cottage industry in the late 1700s. There are only five needle factories in the world, in the Czech Republic, India, England, Japan, and China. The very best needles are made in the British factories, where labor positions are so highly valued that jobs are often handed down from parent to child in the laborer's will! The factories have never become fully automated, so needles have been made in almost the same way for hundreds of years. Skills passed down through the ages have resulted in a quality and pride of workmanship that is unmatched. Due to tough economic times, British factories are beginning to outsource parts of the manufacturing process to other countries. Make sure your package of needles states "Made in England" rather than "Imported into England."

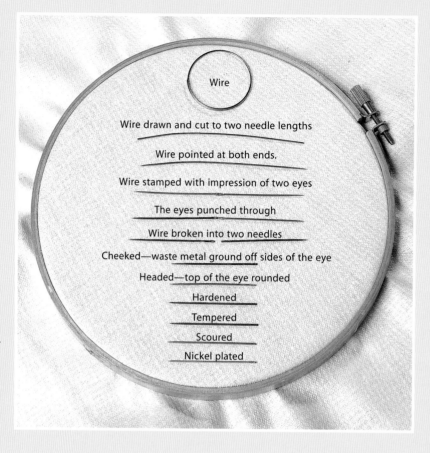

Wire

Wire drawn and cut to two needle lengths

Wire pointed at both ends.

Wire stamped with impression of two eyes

The eyes punched through

Wire broken into two needles

Cheeked—waste metal ground off sides of the eye

Headed—top of the eye rounded

Hardened

Tempered

Scoured

Nickel plated

Needle Test

I examined many of the top brands of quilting needles—all size 10 Betweens. I checked the shaft for thickness and strength; the plating for thickness or the presence of burrs; the point for the proper taper; and the eye for comparative size. I also considered value for money. On a scale of 1 to 10 (1 is poor, 10 is excellent), I assigned a rating to each brand. Here are my results.

Roxanne 9.5	Boye 7.5
Richard Hemming 9	S. Thomas & Sons 7
Foxglove Cottage 8	Clover 6
Mary Arden 8	Bohin 5.5
Colonial 8	Dritz 5
John James 8	Piecemakers 3
JP Coats 8	All platinum & gold 3

All ratings are based on my personal examinations of products I have used

The top needle is an example of a poorly shaped needle. The tip will penetrate fabric easily, then stall at the ridge, causing the quilter unconsciously to push a little harder. Then the ridge will suddenly clear by slipping, causing a momentary lack of control and perhaps the difference between 10 stitches per inch (4 stitches per cm) and 14 stitches per inch (5.5 stitches per cm). A good needle should taper gradually from the eye directly to a point as portrayed below.

How Needles Are Made

All quilting needles, known as Betweens, are made from five-gauge wire that arrives at the factory on spools as big as automobile tires. First, the wire is stretched, which causes it to become thinner. When the wire reaches the specific requirements for the size needle to be made, it is cut into sections the length of two needles. Both ends of each section are ground to a point. Then the center of each section is pressed flat with two dimpled spots. Holes are punched through each of these dimples and the eyes are formed. A laborer then snaps the needle sections in half, separating the two needles. Through a process called "cheeking," waste metal is ground off the sides of the eyes and the top is rounded. The needle as it stands is too weak to be used so it is tempered to harden the metal. It is then prepared for plating by being scoured. Plating is essential as it strengthens the needle and provides a slippery surface so that it can glide easily through fabric. Most needles are plated with nickel, although some use gold or even platinum. The needles are then weighed and counted, and wrapped in packages.

Choosing a Needle

Betweens quilting needles range from the largest, size 1, to the smallest, size 12. The most commonly used sizes are 8 through 12. The larger the number the smaller the needle. In a good brand of needle the diameter of the shaft will proportionately get smaller or larger as the length changes. Therefore, size 12 needles are not only smaller in length but in diameter as well. It is generally agreed the smaller the needle, the easier it goes through the fabric and batting layers of a quilt. Yet there comes a point where the smallness of the needle compromises its strength—a benefit in one area creates a handicap in another. The size of the needle's eye necessarily varies according to the diameter of the needle, so the eye size gets smaller as the needle size gets smaller. In today's market, the eye of a size 12 needle can frequently be smaller than the average quilting thread you are trying to pull through it! The trick is to find the best needle for you, based upon the way in which you sew. For example, I have strong fingers and my stitching is forceful. I cannot use size 12 quilting needles because I bend or snap them when I try to stack my first bunch of stitches! Size 10, or even sometimes size 9, works best for me.

Needle wire on its own is weak. The more it is stretched to make a smaller needle the weaker it becomes. Five-gauge wire has a uniform size, but different factories stretch it to different degrees, and this is a

Sharp Points

Though it is possible to buy gadgets that claim to sharpen dull points, such as special pin cushions filled with grain sand, do not be fooled into using them. The only way to sharpen is to grind to a better point, right? Doing that would mean grinding away the plating, exposing the rough, porous needle wire which will cause even more drag than a dull point. Needles are cheap—simply throw them away when the points dull and start with a fresh one.

Tiare de Tahiti. Made by Roxanne McElroy.
The national flower of Tahiti is quilted in 1/2 inch (1.2 cm) echo.

determining factor in needle quality. If the wire is stretched too much, the needle is so thin that it can be snapped in two with little effort. Another critical point in the making of a needle is the *tempering,* a heating/cooling process that, when done correctly, hardens metals. There is a fine line to tempering needles and it has been a source of pride in the British needle factories for many generations. If a needle is over-tempered it will be too stiff and snap during the pressures of hand quilting. If the needle is under-tempered it is too flexible for the quilter to have ultimate control over the quilting stitch. A needle that snaps during quilting poses a physical danger to the quilter. Small pieces of needle can imbed in a finger or even fly up into the eye! Under pressure, better quality needles will bend instead of snap. A bent or broken needle is useless to quilters.

Plating

All needles must be plated for strength and smoothness, since the raw wires are too coarse to pass through fabrics without catching. While only very obvious flaws are visible to the naked eye, a magnifying glass will show them clearly. The thickness of the plating is impossible to see, however. If the plating, no matter how even, is too thin, the life span of the needle is shortened considerably. A needle with good nickel plating will last for several hours of quilting before the finish starts to wear thin. You can usually tell when the plating begins to wear because of the added drag on the needle as it is pulled through the layers of a quilt. This is a signal that it is time to throw the needle away and start with a fresh one.

Nickel is the most commonly used plating material, but sometimes gold or platinum is used. The finish on those needles is not any smoother than nickel plating. Both are more expensive than nickel—a single platinum needle, for example, can cost as much as an entire pack of nickel-plated needles. In fact, there is only one benefit I can think of to justify the additional expense of these needles— some people have an allergy to nickel that prevents them from quilting. It can cause a severe rash. Gold or platinum needles sometimes can provide relief.

Plating can be eroded by the acidity of a quilter's perspiration. If you notice that your fingers tend to perspire when quilting, you need only change your needles more frequently than other quilters.

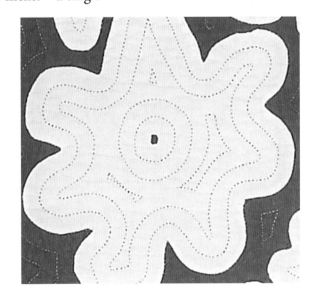

Needle Size

Though some say the smaller the needle, the more skilled the quilter, this is simply not true! After all, a machine sewer would choose a big, strong needle when machine-sewing denim and a small, delicate needle when machine-sewing silk. The same principle holds for hand quilters. With heavy fabric and several seam allowances, only a large needle can penetrate the layers, turn, and resurface without bending or snapping. The key is to use the smallest needle possible to get the job done—that, after all, is why needles are available in such a variety of sizes.

The Wind Travellers. Made by Martha A. Nordstrand, Surprise, AZ.
Hand appliqué with hand embroidered dandelions. A graceful combination of straight-line quilting and freehand quilting. Photograph by Sharon Hoogstraten

Point

A quality needle has a point that tapers very gradually from just below the eye all the way down to the point, so that it moves effortlessly through the layers of a quilt. Some factories take short cuts when making needles. For example, in order to make a size 12 Betweens, they take a size 10, shorten it to the required length, and stick a new point on it (see page 38). This leaves a slight ridge above the point where the point-to-shaft transition occurs. It takes extra force to move that ridge through the layers of a quilt, which means the quilter pushes a little harder. Once the ridge has been passed, the needle tends to slip suddenly causing stitches twice as big as they should be.

The point is the most delicate part of the needle. It is easily damaged when dropped or poorly stored. Often, needles that are carried in metal or flat plastic cases can end up with bent or "jammed" points when they slam against the sides of the case. Barely visible to the naked eye, jammed points are very easy to see through a strong magnifying glass. You can feel them when you are quilting, too. The needle feels blunt as you push it through the layers and tends to catch on quilt fibers when you pull it out.

The Wind-Travelers
A giant Eurasian version of the dandelion called salsify or goat's beard (*Tragopogon dubius*) is one of the most successful wind-travelers in North America. Its seeds have literally blown across mountain ranges, colonizing vast fields of open land in the western United States. This lowly plant has always fascinated me because of its ability to produce flowers, buds and puffballs all at the same time. It is also a very tenacious plant and can adapt and survive even under the most adverse circumstances... I love the simplicity of its form and cheerfulness of its blooms and little Wind-Travelers. This is the fourth in the series of "Noble Elements".

Martha Nordstrand 2007

Jungle Glow. Made by Roxanne McElroy.

The appliqué design in this quilt is very complicated, so simple outline quilting was sufficient to set it off.

Eye

Never believe that the smaller the eye, the better the needle. After all, any time a needle's eye is smaller in diameter than the quilting thread we use, then that needle becomes useless to us. Consider it defective! Some very small needles have large eyes, and those are the ones we should choose. Even large-eye needles, made to help those of us whose eyesight is less than perfect, can pass quality tests with flying colors. I truly believe that most quilters' needle-threading problems stem more from the type of quilting thread they are using than the actual needle eye. The next chapter will explain why.

Improvements in needles will be slight in coming years. I always wished that the industry would offer packages of needles in a variety of different colors so that we could select the one that was most visible against our fabric. So far attempts have been futile. The difficulty seems to be in finding a color material to coat the needle that will remain slippery and not wear off quickly. The coating must also be so thin that it does not fill in the eye too much, causing it to be smaller. Of course, cost will also be an issue with an innovation such as this. Imagine how much easier colored needles would be to find when you drop them on a carpet though! If you ever do find colored needles, make sure they pass all the recommendations given here before you rush to buy them.

Quilter's Workshop

1. Take out all the different brands of needles you have in your sewing basket or buy a selection of brands. Make sure they are all the same size needle. Through a microscope or under a magnifying lens, examine each one for strength, plating, eye, and point construction. Take thorough notes on each brand and then assign a quality rating to each one.

2. Prepare a small "quilt sandwich" of backing, low-loft batting, and a muslin quilt top. Using the needles you rated in the previous exercise, quilt a few stitches with each, noting the differences. Which needle gave you the best stitches with the least effort? Repeat with different needle sizes to determine the size that might be best for you and this particular project.

CHAPTER FOUR

Thread

I deally, early quilters liked to use a coarse cotton thread, generally referred to as "20 count." It was known for its strength and endurance. In reality, however, they used whatever thread they could get hold of, availability being the key factor. Much of the time, regular sewing thread was all they could get at the general store. To strengthen it, they would run the thread through beeswax before quilting with it. Though some quilters still use beeswax, we are fortunate not only to have guidance on which threads will provide the best work, but to have easy access to those products as well. Modern threads come in a multitude of colors and fibers and are available waxed or unwaxed. You can now choose threads to match the purpose of your quilt.

Tricycles and Trains. Made by Roxanne McElroy.
First my mother echo-quilted four times around the outline, leaving bare spots that she did not quite know how to fill. So she flipped the quilt over and appliquéd teddy bears on the back and echo-quilted those four times, too.

Old El Paso. Made by Roxanne McElroy.

Some quilts dictate the quilting design.

Collection of Adele Mozek, The Woodlands, TX

Not All Thread Is the Same

There is an enormous difference between sewing and quilting thread. Quilting thread must be strong in order to withstand the stress put on it by quilting. Sewing thread is 30 to 50 percent weaker than quilting thread and is simply not strong enough for the work it has to do for quilting. We now know that beeswax, painstakingly applied to thread by our ancestors, does not strengthen sewing thread, it merely provides some surface protection and lubrication. If regular sewing thread is used, you must quilt as close as every ½″ (1 cm) so that the strain on each line of quilting is reduced. Even so, I cannot recommend regular sewing thread for quilting.

There is also a great difference between thread manufactured for hand quilting and thread manufactured for machine quilting. Contrary to popular belief, the two are not interchangeable. Think for a moment of how the sewing machine operates. Any given spot on the thread has to be strong enough to be forced down through the quilt top, batting, and backing *just once*. It also has to be soft in texture so it will go through the mechanisms of the machine, without causing excess fuzz. The thread used for hand quilting has to be made differently to be strong enough. An 18″ (45 cm) length of thread is pulled through all the layers of a quilt not once but up to 100 times, with tremendous wear on the entire length of the thread. A good hand-quilting thread is made without a knap and is heavily waxed to prevent excessive knotting or tangling. Heavily waxed threads do not pass through sewing machines smoothly.

Knap

Traditional thread is made of very short lengths of cotton staple, twisted together and wrapped onto a spool. The ends of these short staples stick out of the thread, making it appear "hairy" when viewed under a microscope. The hairs tend to stick out in the exact same direction. This is the thread's *knap*. When the thread is waxed, the knap sticks to the twisted surface. The result is a smoother thread that is easier to pull through fabric and that tends not to tangle.

Because of the knap, the direction in which you pull thread through the fabric is important. If you pull against the knap, you make the staples of the thread stick out even farther, giving your thread a fuzzy quality. As a

Waxing Thread

It certainly is possible for you to take the trouble to pull each strand of your regular unwaxed quilting thread through a chunk of beeswax, just as our ancestors did. But this coats only the outside of the thread and most of the wax is wiped off the first time the thread is pulled through fabric. To get the wax to penetrate the fibers of the thread, you could run an iron over the waxed thread. Even so, it is impossible to get even coverage along the strand. Since factory-waxed threads are readily available and are superior to hand-waxed threads, why would you want to waste your precious quilting time standing at the ironing board?

If you do not match the thread to the fabric, ironing can severely damage the threads in your quilt. Cotton scorches at 360°F (182°C) and polyester melts at 385°F (196°C). Polyester heats up at a rate almost twice as fast as cotton. Quilters who are obsessed with ironing can damage the thread in their quilts by constant ironing, especially if the thread is polyester. The damage is worse with patchwork than appliqué. When both seam allowances are pressed to one side, the running stitch is exposed directly to the iron. Remember, polyester heats twice as fast and does not give a scorch warning before meltdown.

comparison, just think of what would happen if you were to stick a feather through a buttonhole backward. The feather would become ruffled. By pulling against the grain of the knap—referred to in the industry as "runback of twist"—you are roughing up the thread. This makes it more difficult to pull smoothly through the fabric and results in many more tangles, knots, and sudden breaks.

In most cases, the process of wrapping thread onto a spool flattens and smoothes the knap in one direction. If you always knot the end of the thread that comes off the spool *last*, you will be pushing the thread through the fabric in the right direction. Your quilting will go more smoothly and you'll have less tangling. A relatively new trend is the use of Egyptian long-staple cotton, which is wrapped in such a way as to prevent too many hairs from sticking out. This eases the thread's path through fabric.

Thread Construction

In addition to using proprietary cotton staples, each manufacturer has its own secret methods of dyeing, finishing, and wrapping the threads onto spools. There are only two options for twisting the cotton staples together: the manufacturer can twist by rotating to the right or to the left. A right twist is known as an "S" twist and a left twist is referred to as a "Z" twist". Once the staples are twisted together, other finished yarns can be combined with it to form *plies*. A secondary twist, or reverse twist, is used to accomplish this. Hand quilting thread is usually three-ply. (Most threads on the market are two- to four-ply.) More plies mean the thread is stronger, but it is also thicker. A sewing machine can actually add twist to a thread as it runs through mechanisms. For this reason, Z-twist (left twist) threads were designed specifically for the sewing machine. An S-twist thread (right twist) can actually be untwisted inside your machine. Manufacturers often claim that hand quilters can use either type just as effectively. However, my research shows that the traditional S-twist causes far fewer problems with regard to knotting up.

The type of finish used after the thread is constructed can also make a big difference in the thread's ease of use for handwork. The more heavily coated the thread, the less likely it is to break down, get fuzzy, or cause knots during use. There are many terms used to indicate that a thread has been coated, including "glazed,", "glacé," and "waxed." These finishes protect the thread from the constant abrasion of handwork and enhance ply security so that the thread doesn't split as easily at the ends. When the plies of the thread split apart it is almost impossible to thread a needle without a needle threader. If the manufacturer describes a thread as "mercerized," "bonded," or "gassed," this generally means that the thread as been through a heat or chemical process designed to strengthen it or enhance it aesthetically. Be aware, though, that these same processes may shorten the thread's lifespan.

The science behind creating a sewing thread can be mind boggling. Manufacturers must create a thread that is not only beautiful but that has high "sewability." Threads must also have the sufficient strength for their intended application. Ninety-five percent of all threads are sold for industrial and clothing applications. Imagine if the seam on your seatbelt failed during a car accident! There are so many factors involved, it's no wonder that it is almost impossible to have one measuring system to accurately measure all threads. The type of material used alone presents a challenge to measure. Silks, cottons, wools, polyesters and the multitudes of synthetic creations out there all have different specific gravities, densities, strengths, elongation, recovery and dye-ability. Once we add in the number of twists per cm, the direction of twist, the number of plies, and the dozens of finishes and chemical treatments that can be applied, it becomes a mathematical feat to compare each thread on the market!

Thread Weights

So what weight of thread is ideal for hand quilters? I often overhear quilters talk about the threads they use, describing them in terms of thread "weight." Unfortunately, the sizing system used for threads is extremely complicated and, unless you understand the ratios, exact lengths, and number of plies, involved, you probably aren't getting an accurate picture. Some companies may list a ratio number on the spool, such as 40/2. This means that the thread has a cotton count of 40 and is two-ply. The term "NEc" is an indicator of cotton count used for spun threads and refers to the number of hanks of yarn (840 yds) it takes to equal one pound. This formula only works well for two-ply threads because a 40/3 quilting thread is not a 40 weight thread. The same size in a two-ply thread would be more along the lines of a 26 weight thread. Traditional cotton count doesn't apply to any threads that are not "spun," making it difficult to compare sizes among types of thread. Polyester, silk and invisible threads tend to be measured according to "denier count" (Td), instead further complicating things if you are trying to compare.

I have only begun to touch on the math involved in sizing a thread. There are many systems and each manufacturer tends to have its own preferred method, making it near impossible for the average quilter to

Thread Strength Test

Manufacturers like to claim that their thread is the strongest. This is the number one feature they will point out to quilt shop owners at shows. The funny thing is, they measure strength in units that are meaningless to most of us. Who ever heard of microns of ounces, for example? I conducted a very simple test of threads and found that they are all basically the same strength, waxed or unwaxed. I tied identical lengths of thread to the handle of a small pail, suspended from a rail. I added ounces of sand to the pail until the threads broke. They all broke at about the same weight. The exceptions were metallic and monofilament threads, which obviously carried more weight.

Thread Brands

Brand	Thread Name	Material	Colors Available
Heavy Weight Threads			
Superior Threads	Treasure-variegated	Cotton	25
	King Tut	Cotton	100
	Perfect Quilter	Cotton	36
	MonoPoly Invisible	Polyester	2
	Metallic		25
	Nitelite ExtraGlow: Glow in the dark		6
YLI	Quilting	Cotton	
	Colours-variegated	Cotton	
	Jean Stitch	Cotton	
	Silk #30	Silk	
Mettler	Quilting	Cotton	
Gutermann	Quilting	Cotton	50
American & Efird	Signature Cotton Solids	Cotton	18
	Signature Cotton Variegated	Cotton	18
	20's Cotton Solids	Cotton	8
	20's Cotton Variegated	Cotton	10
Sulky	Blendables #30	Cotton	
	Solid Sulky Cotton #30	Cotton	
	Poly Deco	Polyester	
Valdani	Pearl Cotton (size 12)	Cotton	
Medium Weight Threads			
Coats & Clark	Hand Quilting	Cotton	
	Rayon	Rayon	
	Dual Duty Plus: All Purpose	Polyester	
	Dual Duty: Hand Quilting	Cotton/polyester	
Mettler	All Purpose	Polyester	
Gutermann	All Purpose	Polyester	
	Silk	Silk	
YLI	Silk #50	Silk	
	Select	Cotton	
Finishing Touch	#35 Rayon	Rayon	
Sulky	Solid Sulky Cotton #12	Cotton	
	Blendables Sulky Cotton #12	Cotton	
Aurifil	Cotton Mako: Solid colors	Cotton	182
	Cotton Mako: Variegated	Cotton	34
	Cotton Mako '28	Cotton	
Valdani	Home Décor Quilting	Cotton	
Light Weight Threads			
YLI	Soft Touch	Cotton	
	Silk #100	Silk	
	Heirloom	Cotton	
Madeira		Cotton	
Superior Threads	The Bottom Line	Polyester	55
Valdani	All Décor: Hand-dyed variegated	Cotton	
	All Purpose: Vibrant solids	Cotton	
	HomeArt	Cotton	
Coats & Clark	Dual Duty Plus: Lightweight fabrics		
Mettler		Cotton	
	Polysheen	Polyester	
Sulky	Rayon #40	Rayon	
Gutermann	Invisible		
Robinson & Anton	Rayon	Rayon	

Denier	Cotton Count/Ply	TEX Size	Twist	Finish
	30/3			
	40/3			
	30/3			
	Continuous			n/a
	Continuous			
	40/3	40		Glazed
	30/3	50	Z	Mercerized
		90	Z	n/a
567	n/a	63		
	40/3	40		
	40/3	45		Mercerized
	40/3	40		
		40		
	/2			Mercerized
360	/2			Mercerized
	/2			
	50/2	50	S	Mercerized, gassed
	50/3	35	Z	Glazed
	/2	27	Z	Glazed
	/2	27	Z	Mercerized
300	35/2	35		Mercerized
	50/3	35		
318	50/3	35		
	/3	30		
243	/2	27	Z	
	/2	27	S	Glazed
300		27		
	/2		Z	Mercerized
	/2		Z	Mercerized
	50/2		Z	Soft
	28/2			
	/2	25	Z	Mercerized, gassed
	/2	14	Z	Mercerized
124	2 ply	12	Z	
	70/2	11	Z	Glazed
	80/2	14	Z	
		17	Z	Silicone
	50/2	20	Z	Mercerized, gassed
	50/2	20	Z	Mercerized, gassed
	60/2	16.5	Z	Mercerized, gassed
	/2	21	Z	Mercerized
	60/2	19	Z	
240		24		
240	2 ply	24	Z	
	/1	16	n/a	
240		24	Z	

Based on my personal examination of products I have used

Magic of Summer. Made by Ellen Heck.

This quilting design was inspired by a printed fabric. It was stitched entirely in freehand, without marking the quilting lines. The sun rays are stitched in metallic thread.

intelligently discuss differences between brands. There is a universal measuring system that is gaining in popularity and that makes it easier for buyers to select threads suited to their purposes. This is the metric Tex system, a direct numbering system that uses logical whole numbers. In contrast to other fixed-weight systems where the higher the number, the finer the thread, in the Tex system, the higher the number, the coarser the thread.

In the chart on pages 52 to 53, I have attempted to collect data from thread manufacturers to help you compare between companies. Should you receive a supply list for a class that requires a Gutermann thread and your shop only carries Metler, the chart may be able to help you select an appropriate equivalent.

Matching the Thread to the Fabric

When my mother was in high school, she was forced to take Home Economics when she wanted to take Physical Education. She spent the whole semester with an attitude, and, as a result, she did not pay much attention in class. But for some reason, one interesting fact she picked up in Home Economics stuck with her and it turned out to be the most valuable piece of information a quilter could possess.

My mother's teacher told her that if we were to make a garment of polyester, we must use polyester thread. If we used silk fabric, we must use silk thread, with cotton we must use cotton thread, and so on. The teacher reasoned that different fibers have different strengths. If you were to make a garment out of polyester and sew it with cotton thread, you would constantly have to re-sew your seams, because the friction of movement would rub one fiber against the other. The polyester would win every time because it is stronger. If you made a garment of cotton and sewed it with polyester thread, the polyester thread would cut the cotton fiber.

In looking at older quilts, I have seen evidence that this "balance of power" between fabric and thread is very important. Quilts made as recently as the 1950s, when polyester first became popular, began coming back to quilt shops for repairs in the 1980s. In polyester-blend quilts made with cotton threads, the seams need to be re-sewn. In cotton quilts made with polyester threads, cotton patches need to be replaced. My mother's Home Economics teacher was absolutely right!

The three basic types of thread are based on their origin and are animal, plant, and synthetic. Matching the type of thread to the type of

Metallic Thread

I once compromised on one of my quilts by using metallic thread for about an eighth of the quilting, just to see how well it worked. I know that that part of the quilt will one day be cut by the thread, and I will live with my decision to experiment. Remember, metallic thread is exactly what it says—metal. It has much greater strength than fabric and will eventually cut your quilt seriously. For this reason, I can never recommend that your family heirloom quilt be quilted in metallic thread.

Remember not to use more than 18″ lengths of thread while quilting. We tend to hate threading those needles so much that many of my students will cut a yard length if I let them, but then the thread just gets too worn from several hundred passes through the fabric and your arm gets tired from pulling through high into the air. Be sure that the same spot on the thread doesn't stay in the eye of the needle the entire time you are quilting. The needle should slide back on the thread periodically, changing spots, to prevent excess wear in one particular area.

fabric ensures that both products have the same characteristics with regard to shrinkage, strength, and ability to stretch and recover. Think of the reasons you are making your quilt before you choose your thread. If it is a quilt to fit in with a room decor that might change in a few years anyway, or if it is for a child who will love it to death, matching the thread to the fabric may not be important to you. But if you are making an heirloom quilt or want your quilt to have maximum longevity, take care with thread selection.

Using Silk Thread

Some quilters like to appliqué or do patchwork with silk thread when working with cotton fabrics. They feel that since cotton and silk are both natural fibers, they should be interchangeable. They like the way silk thread seems to glide easily through the layers of fabric. But silk thread is not ideal for quilting anything but silk. Silk has a way of elongating over time and it does not recover very well. This means that a process called *smiling* occurs: seams tend to separate and the stitches produce a sort of laddered look. In other words, it looks like the quilter sewed the pieces together too loosely.

Silk thread may appear to be a dream to quilt with because of its slippery nature, but that same feature can work against you. Once you snug your stitch down then let up on the pressure to take another stitch, the thread loosens in the fabric. Moreover, the slipperiness of the thread means that keeping your needle threaded can be extremely frustrating, sometimes tempting you to tie a knot over the eye to keep it in place. The specific spot on the thread that runs through the eye of the needle undergoes more friction than the rest of the thread, since it is folded and wrapped around metal. The thread will oftentimes break at this spot, so it is important to allow the eye to slide up and down the thread as stitches are put into the quilt.

Using Dual-Duty Thread

If polyester is too strong for cotton fabric, then what about quilting thread that has a cotton-wrapped polyester core, such as Coats and Clarks Dual Duty? This thread has not been around long enough to stand the test of time, but it is my opinion that the polyester core will eventually cut through the cotton wrapping and come after your quilt. Dual duty thread was originally designed for sewing machines. Heat builds up in the thread due to friction as the thread rubs against all the metal parts of the machine as it heads for the fabric. The polyester core can melt if too much heat builds up, so manufacturers added an insulating wrap of cotton around the thread. The cotton wrap doesn't last very long, often beginning to rub off inside the sewing machine and producing dust and fuzz that needs to be cleaned out routinely. If you are making a quilt you would like your great-grandchildren to enjoy someday, do not choose dual-duty thread.

Using Decorator Threads

There are many threads other than cotton, polyester, and silk on the market today. Metallic threads are used mostly by machine quilters, but there are a few hand quilters who attempt to use them. It is very difficult to hand quilt with most decorator threads, especially metallic threads, because they tangle and fray. If you are determined to use decorator thread, I suggest you cut lengths of no more than 12″ (30 cm). Put Fray Check—a clear liquid that stabilizes threads from fraying—on your index finger and thumb and pull each length of thread between your fingers to coat it or help smooth it down. All decorator threads must be considered a weakness in a quilt as far as longevity is concerned. Only the quilter can decide whether the creative results outweigh the shortened lifespan.

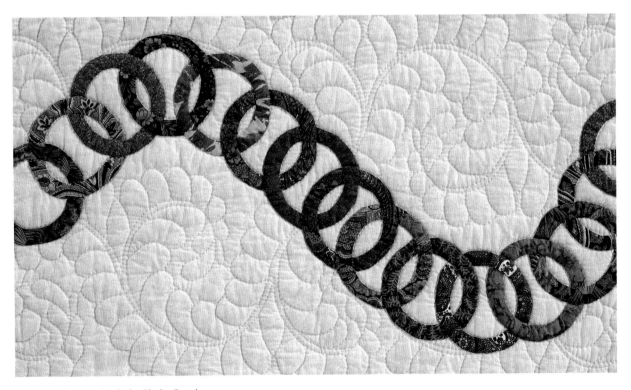

Circles and Stars. Made by Rheba Rozebaum.
The circles are interlocked by hand appliqué. The feathers in the quilting design complement the motion of the circles in the quilt top.

Using Variegated Threads

Threads that change color at measured lengths can be tons of fun to use! This effect results simply from a different way of dyeing the thread and therefore variegated thread is available in cottons, polyesters, silks, and many decorator threads. The quilter cannot control when the thread will change colors and this might make it a little frustrating to use variegated threads for some quilting designs. It helps to know at what lengths the color change happens, such as, every three inches, every 6 inches, etc. If the thread has dramatic color changes from dark to very light, the quilting lines can visually disappear here and there when the light color is passing through. I have seen some rather amazing quilts that used variegated threads quite effectively and they can definitely add extra dimension to certain designs.

Using Invisible Thread

There was a trend for a while to use invisible monofilament threads, designed for use in appliqué on the sewing machine. Invisible thread has also been used in conjunction with cotton thread to give a "hand stitched" look to machine stitches. Having grown up on a South Pacific island and the California coast, I have a great deal of experience with fishing. These threads are not much different from fishing tackle as far as chemical composition is concerned. If you have ever seen fishing tackle that has sat around the garage for ten years, you would be amazed at the oxidization that occurs to fishing line. It turns white, which means it's no longer invisible. It also gets stiff and brittle, and it eventually cracks. Although the invisible threads offered to quilters are not fishing line, they are still a petroleum-based product, and, as such, when open to the air, will oxidize.

Monofilament quilting thread is much thinner than fishing tackle and very fragile. This is easily demonstrated by just breaking some with your bare hands. Compare how it feels with breaking a piece of quality cotton quilting thread.

In addition to the negative properties discussed so far, there are also health and safety concerns in using monofilament thread in quilts intended for use by children or that will come in contact with cherished family pets.

Final Analysis

Thread can be a singular source of frustration during quilting. I have narrowed the entire market down to two threads that I use almost exclusively in my quilts: YLI hand quilting cotton and Superior Threads

Treasure. Still, any thread can be used to make a quilt; it is up to each quilter to balance such considerations as artistic effect, ease of use, or cost against longevity. I admire all those quilters who hand sew quilts for their grandchildren to love and drag around. I can make a really good argument, however, that if the right thread and fabrics are assembled, little Joey will be able to drag that treasured quilt around a couple years longer! When it comes right down to it, though, if your thread is driving you crazy, then hand quilting is not as much fun as it should be! As with all quilting tools and materials, make the compromises you need in order to enjoy the process of making your quilt.

Quilter's Workshop

Make a fabric sandwich of muslin top, low-loft batting, and muslin backing. Gather together samples of regular sewing thread, waxed quilting thread, unwaxed quilting thread, and an assortment of metallics and monofilament threads. You may even want to run regular thread through beeswax to test that, too. Quilt a little with each thread to compare differences in workability and strength. Look at each thread under a magnifying glass before using and then after it has been pulled through the quilt a few times to observe the wear.

CHAPTER FIVE

Thimbles

When we think of thimbles, many of us remember our mothers or grandmothers sitting quietly and working on a delicate piece of needlework. The first image that comes to mind is of the elegant, lacy sterling silver thimbles they used to shield their fingers from needle puncture. Sterling silver was a sign of quality, and women took care of their thimbles as though they were fine pieces of jewelry. And why not? Those sterling silver thimbles originally cost just as much. Today thimbles come in a variety of shapes and colors. Some are functional; others are strictly collector items. Most quilters have a collection of thimbles that were hoped-for solutions to one source of aggravation or another. We are all searching for the perfect thimble.

***Les Sirenes* (The Mermaids).** Made by Roxanne McElroy.
Waves cover the quilt, and the unique quilted fish scattered throughout add interest. Notice the appliquéd fish on the backing, perfectly stitched to correspond with the quilting design on the quilt top.

The Paddle

Instead of a thimble, some quilters use a little instrument that looks like a tiny tennis racket with a spoon handle attached. House of Quilting's Paddle is simply a dimpled disk with a small handle. It is meant to be held in the hand and the stitches are made by rotating the wrist. It was originally developed to help quilters who, because of arthritis, have difficulty pinching their fingers together to make running stitches. I've tried the Paddle and have worked with it long enough to master the technique, but I found it to be very stressful on my wrist and the back of my hand. At a time when quilters are increasingly concerned about carpel tunnel syndrome, I admit my fears about this tool. Even so, one thing I find annoying is the time wasted with the Paddle—you use it to stack stitches, then you have to put it down while you pull the needle through and reset it, only to pick the Paddle up again to execute the stitches.

How the Muscles in the Quilting Hand Work

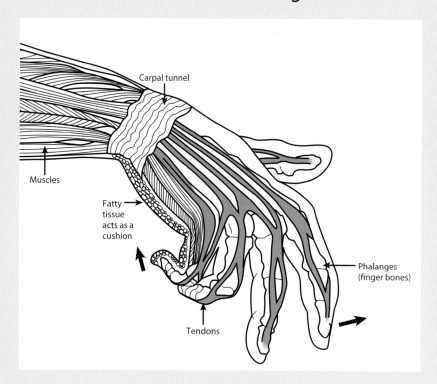

Because of the muscular-skeletal structure of the hand, it is easy to strain the hand if quilting incorrectly. The term *strain* covers a variety of conditions. Each is caused by constant repetition of a particular hand movement, especially those made under suboptimal conditions and in poor positions. Irritation of the tendons, shown in blue, is a strain that is common among quilters. It is caused by pressure on the median nerve and tendons as they pass through the *carpal tunnel,* a crosswise ligament at the front of the wrist. Tendons and muscles cause bones to move by contracting (shortening) and releasing (returning to normal). Notice the placement of the tendons on the finger bones. They run lengthwise. If you were to pull or contract them near the carpal tunnel, the fingers would move in the direction of the arrows. The human hand does not have muscles that cause the tips of the fingers to move sideways. Quilters who push incorrectly from the side are using a gross motor movement emanating from the carpal tunnel area and the elbow, causing undue strain in those areas as they attempt to control a highly skilled action such as the quilting stitch. Quilters who have been forced to use the very tip of their fingers due to poorly shaped thimbles are jamming the finger joints. This can cause early forms of arthritis and can certainly aggravate preexisting conditions.

Choosing a Thimble

Needlework thimbles, like the ones our grandmothers wore, are not at all suited to the art of quilting for many reasons. Most have walls too thin to withstand the extreme pressure required to penetrate the multiple layers of a quilt. When there are four very tiny stitches already on the needle and the quilter is trying for a fifth, the pressure on the needle is enormous! Pushing a needle through all those tiny stitches is very hard on a thimble with thin walls. The quilter is in grave danger of being wounded.

My mother, Roxanne, was quilting in her Lazy Boy chair one night while I was home from school on winter break. An ear-piercing squeal brought us all downstairs to her aide when we realized she had punctured a quilting needle through her leather thimble and it was stuck in the bone of her finger. My dad went out to the garage and grabbed a pair of needle-nose pliers and pulled it out for her. A very long discussion ensued on the design flaws of thimbles. Mom showed me all the thimbles she had collected and tried. I set about to study thimbles and I have spent a great deal of time and effort searching for thimbles and evaluating them. I would like to share my findings with you to help you make the right choice. As you read, keep in mind these five factors: glove-like fit; puncture-proof quality; rounded at finger pad; deep dimples; and beauty as an accessory you will wear often!

Evaluating Thimble Dimples

The size and depth of the dimples on the outside of a thimble play an important part in quilting. This is because the dimples affect your control of the needle, and for That Perfect Stitch, absolute control is critical. If the blunt end of the needle has to slide around searching for a sparsely placed dimple, control is impossible. Similarly, if the needle slips out of a dimple that is too shallow or catches on one that is too deep, control is lost. It is possible for the dimples to be too deep. The eye of the needle has to be able to pivot somewhat within the dimple; dimples that are too deep can put excess wear on the thread as it folds through the eye or, in some cases, crack the eye off the needle! There is an entire science to proper placement, angle and shape of each individual dimple. Dimples must not only be deep but they must be evenly concave and angled at 90 degrees to the face of the thimble.

Comparing Thimbles

Flat-top thimbles force you to push . . .

. . . with the top of a finger, like this.

A well-designed thimble allows you to push . . .

. . . with the ball and pad of the finger, like this . . .

Not from the top, like this . . .

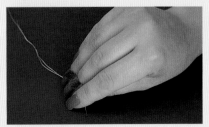
. . . and not sideways, like this.

Return to M'Zima, Waiting for the Rain. Made by Patricia Harrington, Spring, TX.
The background quilting follows the curved piecing to accent the movement—of seasons and of the animals. The rest of the quilting accents the animals moving toward the springs at M'Zima in the center. The quilter used an overlay of a piece of black fabric, then placed the animals, and cut the black fabric away as she appliquéd.

Minimizing Stress on the Fingers

While I was studying thimbles, I was also studying Biomedical Science at Texas A&M University. I launched myself into an in-depth study of anatomy and talked with orthopedic surgeons. It quickly became very clear how important it is for a quilter to use a thimble that allows her to push the needle through the layers of a quilt at the *correct angle*. Our finger joints actually act as shock absorbers. The bone ends are covered with cartilage and, when working properly, form a sealed container for the vital fluids that lubricate the cartilage and so lessen the friction when we use or bend our fingers. Our fingers are meant to bend only one way. Repeated pressure to the side of a joint—which happens when a needle is pushed at an incorrect angle—will eventually result in irritation to the joint and can lead to premature arthritis. One form of arthritis is caused by loss of lubrication in the joints. The bone ends rub against each other, causing irritation and inflammation. It is not uncommon for quilters to experience pain and stiffness in the elbows, shoulders, neck, and back from lengthy quilting sessions the day before!

There are several thimbles on the market that have ridged flat tops. All of these are faulty in design because they cause the quilter to use the tip of the finger—rather than the ball and pad of the finger—to push the needle. The muscles in the finger simply do not work in this direction. It is an extremely stressful angle, not to mention inefficient for quilting. The finger joints are jammed at each push of the needle, causing inflammation. Wrong angles also cause the entire arm to work in a gross motor movement instead of the more dexterous fine motor movement that the hand is capable of. Flat-top thimbles usually have a grid of dimples at the top, but in an effort to gain more control over the needle and to protect the finger, most quilters rely on the ridge around the top to catch the needle. This causes the thimble to cant, giving the quilter calluses around the finger where the edge of the thimble rubs.

Evaluating Thimble Strength

Most thimbles are not built for the strength it takes to push the needle through the layers of a quilt. The Tailors Thimble is one of these. Designed in China hundreds of years ago, The Tailors Thimble is made up of a band of metal with dimples that slides on around the finger to protect the ball or pad.

The weakest thimbles I have found are made of leather. And, because they lack strength, these are the most dangerous types of thimble to use. Leather simply cannot withstand the pressures the better quilters exert, and needles puncture quilting fingers regularly. A leather thimble will only last a good quilter about a month, and comparatively speaking, they are very expensive. Some manufacturers, in an effort to increase the life span of leather thimbles, insert a metal pad into the leather. What happens, though, is that because this metal plate is smooth, the eye of the needle slides to the edge of it and right off into the fingers. The one benefit of a leather thimble is that the quilter can avoid joint damage by using the ball of the finger properly.

Thimbles and Fingernails

My next stop in researching thimbles was a Beauty School to consult with a fingernail expert. Many women today choose to wear long nails or artificial nails. The simple act of drumming the nails on a table causes shock waves to travel up through the nail bed to the root of the nail. When pushing a thimble, the pressure is much greater. If the trauma is heavy enough, the nail grows out with ridges across it. At the very least, the nail becomes brittle or weak and tends to break or split easily, making it difficult for women to achieve a well manicured look. Being crammed repeatedly into a thimble also cuts off oxygen to the nail, adding to this condition.

I have come across a soft gray rubber thimble, designed to accommodate long fingernails. It has a slanted top that is gridded. The thimble works well to push the needle through the layers of the quilt, but when you release the pressure to grab the needle, you often find that the needle has stuck into the thimble, pulling the stitches back out!

Even if you are not concerned about keeping long or well manicured nails, keep in mind that even short nails get jammed inside flat-top thimbles, causing discomfort and making it difficult to stitch. Even the fleshy tip of a finger is rounded to varying degrees depending on your cultural heritage and genetic makeup.

Thimble Size

The single most frustrating problem with the thimbles on the market is that most of them come in a limited size range. When my mother could not find a thimble to fit, even a bad thimble, she had to resort to leather ones. Leather thimbles restrict movement—it feels as though you are trying to quilt with a glove on. And, as we have seen, they are simply not strong enough for quilting. A good thimble should fit the very tip of the finger only. It should not come anywhere near the knuckle, let alone cover it. If your range of motion is even slightly limited you will subconsciously adjust for the discomfort and begin pushing from an angle that is not orthopedically correct. Further, a good thimble should not rotate in the least around the finger, especially 15 to 20 minutes after the finger has warmed up then shrunk a little.

A thimble I thought would be pretty good was one made of plastic with an open front. The open front accommodated long fingernails, and the dimples were nice and deep. Unfortunately, this thimble comes in only two or three sizes, none of which fit my mother. I was told to put it in a pan of boiling water. This would supposedly soften the plastic enough to mold the thimble to her finger; when the plastic cooled, it would hold that shape. We tried a couple of times and could not get it to work. Either nothing at all happened or the thimble ended up a blob of plastic in the bottom of my pan. That is probably my fault though—I cook like that, too.

Rating Thimbles

	Puncture proof	Precision fit	Well-done dimples	Orthopedically correct	Beauty
Roxanne's thimble	5	5	5	5	5
Metal flat-top thimble	2	1	2	1	2
Leather thimble	2	3	1	5	3
Porcelain thimble	4	2	2	1	5

The most important thing
to look out for when trying
on a thimble is that it not
budge on your finger at all.
A thimble that fits snugly
will not cause joint stress
and will allow for complete
and total needle control.
Remember that fingertips
can change size with new
medications, heavy exercise,
standing for long periods or
even with dramatic weather
changes. Fit your thimble to
your finger after 15 to 20
minutes of quilting, when
excess fluids have drained
away and your finger is at
its true size.

Roxanne's Thimble

My research into thimbles over several years left me feeling frustrated and my mother with sore fingers. I could tell that my mother was even embarrassed that her fingers were too big to even try on most of the thimbles I brought home. I needed to find a solution to the problem so that my mother could continue this new passion of hers. Through all the research I did I had come up with a personal set of criteria for the ultimate thimble.

The thimble had to not only be big enough to fit my mother's finger but it had to fit like a glove. I watched a lot of quilters try on thimbles at quilt shows and test the fit by simply dumping their hands upside down and shaking to see if the thimble fell off easily. In my mind, this thimble had to fit my mother perfectly at all times. I didn't want it to rotate even a tiny bit around her finger as she quilted. When looking at human anatomy in a seated quilting position, it was clear that the pad of the finger was the correct area to be pushing a needle from. Yet the pad of the finger is rounded and I decided that the thimble, too, should be rounded at that spot. It should not be flat or designed with a ridge right at the area most needed for pushing.

The ultimate thimble should have plenty of dimples. The dimples should be angled correctly around the curves of the finger. They should be concave in shape instead of just punched straight down into the thimble. This way, they can protect the eye of the needle from excess stress yet keep it in place as the quilter pivots the needle from a 90-degree angle to a 180-degree angle without having to sneak her thumb up to keep it in place.

No matter what material the thimble is made from, it had to be strong enough to handle quilting without being punctured. It would be even nicer if it was a material that would last a lifetime, since the perfect thimble seemed to be such an ordeal to find! Depending on the type of materials involved, the open front is a critical feature to allow the nail bed to breath and to allow air to circulate within the tight quarters.

My mother made things a bit more difficult by insisting that the thimble also had to be pretty. We argued repeatedly over the balance between beauty and functionality.

Since I never found a thimble on the market that encompassed more than two of our desired features, my mother and I decided we would design our own. We named it the Roxanne Thimble, and it is shown in the photographs throughout this chapter. After making one just for Roxanne, we discovered that she wasn't the only frustrated quilter out there who needed a better thimble. We began producing other sizes which only led us to more studies about genetics and the varieties of shapes that are evident in the human finger. It was a real challenge to produce a product that could fit 95 percent of quilters to the degree that our original model fit my mother. Roxanne's Thimble is now manufactured by Colonial Needle Company and is available in a range of materials, sizes, and styles to help every quilter find that perfect fit!

Quilter's Workshop

Try on thimbles in varying sizes to find the one that is right for you. Make sure that it is comfortable, but that it does not fall off easily or rotate on your finger. Take a small "quilt sandwich" of batting, backing, and quilt top with you to the store and try out the thimble you think fits best.

CHAPTER SIX

Frames and Hoops

We realized very early in our quilt history that it was beneficial to keep the layers of the quilt taut during the quilting process in order to avoid pleats and puckers in the finished work. There was a variety of ways to do this but generally it involved building some kind of frame. The quilter would fasten together strips of wood the size of the piece to be quilted. The slats were about 1″ (2.5 cm) thick, 2″ (5 cm) wide, and up to 108″ (275 cm) long. Each slat had a narrow strip of fabric nailed or stapled to it onto which the edges of the quilt backing were basted. This method required heavy basting and often provided a social occasion, where women would gather for a meal and help a friend baste her quilt.

Jacobean Vines. Made by Margaret Illions, Las Vegas, NV.
Beautiful appliqué flowers complimented by quilting done in concentric circles. Shown displayed on my favorite frame, the Grace Z44 quilt frame from Grace Frame Company. Also shown on page 78. The quilt is photographed in the Grace Frame. The quilt in the hoop, above, **Ia Orana** *by Dierdra McElroy, uses outline quilting of a pattern in the fabric onto the white muslin background.*

I once heard a fascinating story of early quilters and their frames. To save space, a quilter would suspend her frame from the ceiling by hooks and pulleys so she could raise it when it was not in use. This was usually done over dining tables or beds because of the space required for a quilt frame of such dimensions. It is a very exciting image for me to think of looking up from my table or bed to see the back of my current quilt-in-progress! I have often fantasized about installing a frame this way, but it would probably be for sake of conversation only. I tend to lean heavily on my quilt frame and would be in grave danger of knocking a hole in a wall or breaking a window!

C-Clamp Frames

Since the earliest days of quilting, frames have not really changed much. They were typically made of 1″ × 4″ (2.5 cm × 10 cm) lengths of wood. The wood was put together in almost the exact dimensions of the quilt itself and then held together with C-clamps (metal tools shaped like the letter C with a foot that screws down onto another foot, securing two objects together). The quilt top, batting, and backing were put together and then placed over the frame and tacked down to the poles. There was no basting to be done, which is a big advantage, but this type of frame took up phenomenal amounts of space. Imagine a king size quilt laid out flat in your living room! Frames like this are still fairly common, since many quilters can sit around them, stitching together. A disadvantage is that the quilting is done from the outside in, which can cause irreversible puckers at the center of the quilt if the quilters are not careful.

Installing the Quilt

When using a traditional C-clamp frame, enlist the help of friends to install the quilt.

1. The pole dimensions should be no larger or slightly smaller than the quilt dimensions. Measure from the outside of one pole to the outside of the other pole when the frame is assembled.
2. Put the poles together and secure the joints with C-clamps.
3. Spread the backing over the frame face down, making sure it is square and not distorted. Tack it to the frame with quilting thumb tacks.
4. Next, place the batting over the frame making sure an equal amount of batting is hanging over each edge. It is best to make your batting slightly larger than the quilt itself, since the quilting process will shrink it slightly. You can either tack it down with new tacks or, if you have helpers, remove the first tacks one by one from the backing and place them over the batting and backing.
5. Finally the top goes on face up. Center it and tack it down to the frame. The frame can then either be placed on stanchions (stands), or suspended from the ceiling.

Basting

The quilt can either be basted before going into the frame, in which case all three layers are tacked onto the frame simultaneously, or it can be basted after installation. If the quilt is not basted, do not remove it from the frame until it is completely quilted. If you choose to baste first, the best way to baste is from the center out, thus drawing the wrinkles out to the edges to be released. Make a basting line from the center out to each side of the quilt, then baste from the center out to each corner. From here, continue basting lines from center out running between the lines already done. Personally I wouldn't leave more than 3″ (8 cm) between basting lines radiating outward. Thorough basting before installing a quilt into a quilt hoop or frame will ensure a finished quilt that is square and flat upon completion.

Sawhorse Frames

Another basic type of frame that has been traditionally used by quilters is the sawhorse frame. This frame is more widely used than the one described above because it is easy to make and takes up less space. Similar in construction to the sawhorses carpenters use, the frame is a little taller—36″ (90 cm) rather than 28″ (70 cm). Two sawhorses are set up opposite each other and 2″ × 2″ (5 cm × 5 cm) quilt poles are nestled into notches cut into the crossbars, equidistant from one another. The length of the poles vary depending on the size of the quilt to be worked on. The tension on the quilt is limited to one turn of the pole. Quilters can sit together on either side of the frame and, when finished working for the day, the poles can be lifted out of the sawhorses, rolled up together, and stored in a closet until the next session.

Basting and Installing the Quilt

This is a primitive frame that requires heavy basting before the quilt is put into the frame. When using a two-pole sawhorse system, the best method is to baste as you roll the quilt into the frame. This way, the quilt gets basted without the space required to lay it flat.

1. Attach a long piece of folded muslin to the back pole. It must be at least the length of the quilt being installed. This can be done with a staple gun or large flat-head tacks. The muslin strip will stay on for multiple quilts.

2. Mark the center of the back pole by measuring the length and then dividing that length in half. Find the center of your quilt backing by folding it in half lengthwise. Pin the center of the quilt backing to the muslin strip attached to your pole at its center spot. Gently smooth and pin the backing to the muslin strip, starting at the center point and working out. When you finish one side it might be wise to measure from where the fabric ends to the end of the pole. Make sure that same distance is left on the other side after it is

Quick Baste

Some quilters have come up with ingenious ways to baste their quilts into frames. One quilter I know insists it is less work basting the layers of a quilt together if the frame is laid across the seats of chairs. She lays down on the floor underneath the frame and bastes it! Another quilter stands the quilt frame up in a wide doorway and recruits a friend to stand on the back side of the quilt to grab the basting needle and direct it back through to the front of the quilt! Both quilters claim their methods serve to avoid back pain. Personally, I agree the most painless way to baste a quilt is to stand the frame in a doorway. But I would prefer to recruit two friends to stand on either side of the frame to baste, while I supervise with a glass of Coke and a lap full of appliqué!

King Kamehameha. Made by Roxanne McElroy.
*Here the sun is accentuated with diagonal rays. The body is echo-quilted
to give it an inward energy.*

pinned and before the backing is basted down. Once the backing is attached to the pole and centered, you can baste it to the muslin strip and remove the straight pins.

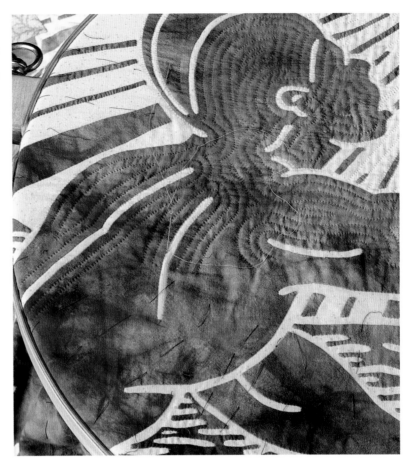

3. Repeat Step 1 with the opposite side of the quilt backing. Make sure that the same distances are kept from the fabric edge to the ends of the poles. Baste securely after pinning and measuring.

4. Roll the quilt backing onto the back pole until the center of the backing is reached. (The easiest way to find these center points is to fold the fabric or batting in half lengthwise, then in half crosswise. The center fold is also the center point. Temporarily mark them.) It is vital that you watch the fabric on the poles as you roll. The overlapping edges must be right on top of each other with edges matching.

5. Repeat Step 3 but roll the backing onto the front pole. Again watch the edges as they overlap onto the pole; they should match exactly. If they do not you need to re-baste the backing to the pole and measure carefully.

6. Drape the batting over the quilt frame with the center point of batting matching the center point of the quilt backing. (It can be very helpful, depending on the batting you choose, to remove the batting from its package and lay it out flat over a bed or on the floor overnight to let the wrinkles settle.)

7. Drape the quilt top over the quilt frame with the center point matching the center points of the batting and backing.

8. Begin basting the quilt at the center point. Smooth the top flat and baste using a very long needle and any cotton thread. Run a line of basting stitches to each edge from the center always working outward. Continue running basting lines across the quilt, mindful of quilt edges as they roll. Begin quilting at the center working out. Continue running basting lines across the quilt from the center out every 3″ (8

cm) until you get very close to a pole. Then, roll the basted part of the quilt onto the pole, exposing new areas to quilt. As you roll, make sure the edges of the quilt overlap exactly, to ensure the quilt is basted squarely. Once half the quilt is basted, roll it back to the center carefully, and work on the other half from the center out.

Take care not to roll the quilt into the frame too tightly. If the quilt is "drum-tight," you have no room at all to warp the layers over the needle to achieve That Perfect Stitch and you may be inadvertently warping the squareness of your quilt.

Full-Size Frames

A two-pole frame functions like a large quilt hoop on legs and cannot fairly be considered an effective frame system. The three-pole frame was introduced about 75 years ago. In a good three-pole system there is no need for basting. The quilt top and batting are rolled together onto one pole; the backing is rolled onto a second pole; and the whole quilt is then pulled forward and wrapped around the front or third pole. Basting has always been one of my least favorite things to do, so you can imagine my excitement upon discovering the three-pole system years ago. The Grace Company makes a frame known as the Z44 (see page 70) to which engineers have added a fourth pole option! This way, the top and batting each have their own separate poles. With this quilting system a quilt will always lay perfectly flat upon completion!

Choosing a Frame

In the late 1980s, a quality quilting frame could easily cost more than $1300, but you can get a good one for half of that these days. There are several frames on the market and some can mean a serious investment in your quilting. Before you make that investment do your homework!

Height

A quilt frame should be high enough that when your upper arm is at the side of your body, and your forearm is extended out, the pole of the frame fits right into the bend of the arm. Most frames have tilt features that might help tailor the height to your body. (Make sure you sit down at the frame before making adjustments.) Some of the pivot points for the tilting cause the front pole to drop significantly. This means in order to take advantage of the tilt you have to give up the comfort level of the height. You will find yourself leaning sideways to reach under the frame.

When quilting, it is very important to use a good quality orthopedic, height-adjustable chair. I prefer one without arms because I find I don't rest my arms and they just get in my way. Adjust the frame and the chair in conjunction with one another to provide your back with lumbar support and prevent you from hunching over your frame at a 90 degree angle that will cause neck and back pain.

As our quilting designs change angles and direction, we tend to warp our bodies, stretching and straining, to reach the lines. Your stitches will suffer if you are even a bit out of that small window of correct range of motion. Make sure the frame you choose adjusts quickly and easily, without you needing to rotate knobs or use tools. If the adjustments take too much effort, you will find it easier to just stretch and strain than adjust the frame.

Tension

A quilt should never be put into a frame drum-tight. That Perfect Stitch can only be achieved when the fabric is loose enough to manipulate around your needle. You will quickly discover that adjusting the tension on your frame in fine degrees is a valuable feature. To achieve an even tension along the length of the poles a ratchet system is most effective. This takes out the "human factor" of hand-rotating your poles. The larger the diameter of the ratchets, the finer the degree of tensioning available. Another factor is how many actual ratchets are on the wheel. Anything less than 30 notches will leave you wishing you could adjust "in-between." Make sure that the ratchet wheel locks into place securely by wiggling the poles back and forth.

Sturdiness

In recent economic times, all manufacturers have sought to find ways to decrease costs. Quilters also demand lower prices, and they are often unwittingly giving up valuable features for their dollar. One of those critical features is stability. Twenty years ago the best quilt frames were heavy duty solid wood frames that elephants could sit on. As I have said, I tend to lean heavily on my frame as I quilt and it makes me very unhappy to feel the frame giving way under my weight. There is a delicate balance between using thinner woods, synthetic materials, and engineering the shape to maintain balance. Some companies achieve this with wide bases that can get in the way of your knees or feet. Certainly a top heavy frame will never do, so make sure your frame choice has stable design features.

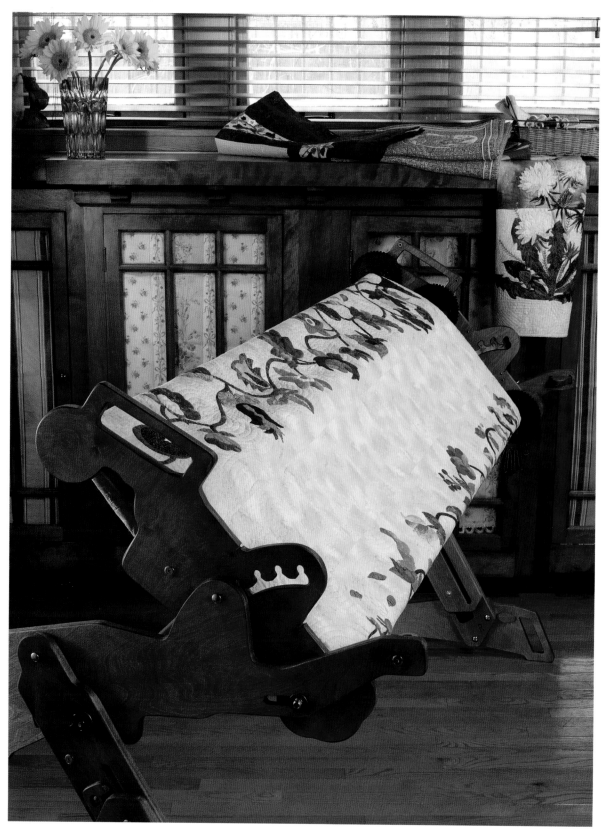

Jacobean Vines. Made by Margaret Illions, Las Vegas, NV.
Beautiful appliqué flowers complimented by quilting done in concentric circles. Shown displayed on my favorite frame, the Grace Z44 quilt frame from Grace Frame Company. Also shown on page 70.

The types of poles available for your frame are an important consideration. I found through experience that solid wood poles tend to bow with time and humidity. So my frame of choice was one that had laminated wood poles for strength and rigidity. In recent years, almost all of the companies have switched to aluminum or extruded polymers. This change makes for a lighter weight frame that is less costly to ship. It also eliminates bowing with age. They still can be damaged, chipped or dented if the quilter isn't careful. Most frames come with poles of varying lengths to accommodate quilts of different sizes.

Size

Since most of us do not have an entire room dedicated to our quilting, space is always an important consideration when choosing a full-size frame. Standard frames measure 34″ (86 cm) deep, but some are available in a narrow-profile that only measures 28″ (70 cm). If you are going to be the only one quilting at the frame (versus group quilting), then the narrow profile is a more efficient use of space. After all, there is only just so far that your arms can reach across the frame before your shoulders round, and the rest is just wasted space. Some frames dismantle quickly for space but I have to say that in my experience you are kidding yourself if you think that you will put up a frame "just long enough to get this quilt done" and then take it down! Every single hand quilter I have talked to admits that her frame has become a part of her decor. My biggest piece of advice to you would be to shop for a frame as you would a piece of furniture. Require the same functionality as well as beauty from your frame that you would look for in a sofa or dining table.

The diameter of the poles in your frame do make a difference. Depending on the material they are made from the diameter can affect the strength and longevity of your poles. If the diameter is too large, such as 4"x 4" (10 cm x 10 cm), then once the quilt is wrapped several times around the pole the thickness can become so wide that you end up leaning sideways to get your arm under and up to the quilt surface. This can definitely result in neck, back and hip discomfort with time. The Grace Company reports that, for this reason, their poles are now only 1½" (4 cm) in diameter.

Finish

I cannot tell you how many times I have heard quilters say they are not going to spend the $65 to have their frame stained and sealed because their husbands can just do it for them. Even if your husband is a true handyman, the time and effort it takes to get him to do it in a timely

Beauty

My motto has always been "Beauty in Form and Function." The two must go hand in hand and one is useless without the other. Jasmine Heirlooms makes a three-pole frame that is stunning in beauty. It has scroll-worked legs and a beautiful stain. Do not let beauty be the main indication of function. This frame is closer to a sawhorse design. Norwood and Hinterburg's frames are darkly stained and very beautiful. The Grace Company can stain your new frame any shade you would like to match your decor or it can come to you unfinished if you would like to stain it yourself. Pleasant Mountain also makes a beautiful upper-end frame that runs a close second to the Grace Frame in functionality.

Lap Quilting

Georgia Bonesteel gets my MVP award for single-handedly making the quilting process portable. She developed a method of quilting called *lap quilting*, which is done by quilting one good size square at a time and then attaching the quilted squares together with French-Fold seams. This method convinced quilters that they could do entire quilts in a hoop, and it was a huge stepping stone to portability for all of us.

manner is wasting the time you can be spending quilting! Furthermore, frame manufacturers have nailed down the exact processes and chemicals to finish the frame so that no acids, dyes, or other chemicals will leach onto your quilt over time. I can't stress enough how much easier it is to just let the manufacturer do it for you. You will have a gorgeous ready-to-use frame upon arrival at your home with no disasters down the road!

Quilting Hoops

A full-size quilt frame with a ratcheting system and at least three poles is the ideal quilting system. Unfortunately, not all quilters have the ways or means to place a large frame in their homes. In other words, a compromise is in order. I use a hoop to quilt all my small pieces and find it very convenient for my busy lifestyle. Many quilters choose to use hoops because they can be rotated in order to quilt always in a favorite direction. Others choose them because they want to quilt in the same room with their families.

Hoops on Floor Stands

Most frame companies also offer hoops mounted on floor stands. These types of hoops not only make great display pieces for any room, they allow you to keep quite a bit of the quilt off your lap while you work. The biggest advantage to a hoop on a floor stand is for anyone with orthopedic challenges, such as shoulder, neck, back, or any other issues with the arms. The hoop and quilt essentially float before you and eliminate the need to hold, pin down, or counterbalance the hoop while stitching. This type of system can save someone that might otherwise have to stop hand quilting.

When searching for the perfect floor-stand hoop, there are several factors you should explore before purchasing. During the lifetime of your new hoop you may want to use it both for smaller projects like wall hangings and for quilts as large as king size. Make sure that the base of the entire system is sufficient to prevent the hoop from being top heavy. If it wobbles, tilts, or falls over with a large, heavy quilt as you try to rotate the hoop during stitching, it will annoy you to death. Or worse, you might begin adjusting your body and feet to stabilize the hoop, defeating the purpose of the stand. I know one quilter who made gorgeous batik sandbags to weigh down her base and solve her problem!

A hoop has to be attached to the stand in some way, often via a flat bar positioned beneath the hoop. Whatever form of attachment is used, it must leave room for the quilter to easily stick an underneath hand under the hoop, and maneuver that hand without obstructions. I always tell my students to put a hand underneath with the back of the hand flat against the bar/arms/base and stretch their fingers up towards the hoop. If your fingers can stretch up past the plane of the hoop then I wouldn't recommend that system. For ultimate comfort, I like to see about 4 to 5 inches (10 to 12 cm) between the hoop edge and the base it is attached to.

It is essential that your hoop be able to rotate and tilt in all directions—easily and quickly. If you know you have to stop, loosen knobs, bend the frame, then, if you are like most quilters, you will just decide to suffer through and shift your body rather than deal with the hoop's mechanisms. For this reason, I recommend hoops that have a ball joint rather than an adjustment mechanism. The ball joint allows the hoop to tilt to any angle and rotate 360 degrees smoothly and quickly when the quilting line changes direction. To achieve That Perfect Stitch, your body must be in an orthopedically correct position and you must be comfortable. If your hoop forces you to change positions, your stitches will suffer for it, as will your body in the long run. Many rotating hoops seem to have one spot that will not tilt when rotated in that direction and that can become very frustrating. Test a prospective hoop out as if test-driving a new car. Tilt and turn the hoop every imaginable way!

Jasmine Heirlooms has a very nice system called the EasySpinner Stand, photographed on page 74. The hoop is available in Maple or Oak and is mounted on a ball joint, allowing it to tilt and rotate at all angles. The bars that hold the hoop up off the center post are curved and leave plenty of room for the underneath hand to do its work. The post itself is mounted to a large oval platform to stabilize the entire system. A ratchet system allows the post to adjust quickly from 90 degrees to flat on the floor, letting you raise or lower the overall head to match the chair you are sitting in. The EasySpinner Stand is beautiful and displays well in the home. The drawback is cost; you will spend almost as much for this stand as you would for a basic full-size quilt frame.

The most state-of-the-art system on the market is the Grace Hoop2 from The Grace Company (pictured on page 84). This non-traditional stand takes up a bit more room than the Jasmine EasySpinner but the base slides easily under a sofa or Lazy Boy chair so that the quilter can get up close to the quilt. The arm bends and swings away for easy exit from a chair, and there are holes and posts for tool storage. The center post can easily mount a swing arm lamp for direct light on the quilt. The system is super sturdy, it folds up easily, and has a built-in handle for better

Hand-Held Hoops

I have seen quilters go to their local quilting bees with a bed-size quilt dumped into a laundry basket. They have a 140 (35 cm) or 160 (40 cm) hoop in one area of the quilt that they lift out and work on! It obviously works for them. The disadvantage to this system is that you are always stuck with lots of quilt in your lap that could get quite warm, depending on where you live and the time of year. Trying to rotate the hoop can also be quite cumbersome. The additional weight of a bed-size quilt helps weight down the hoop, as if it has a base. But the moment a smaller project is installed, the quilt flops around unmercifully in the hoop, making precision stitches impossible. I have witnessed many a quilter in my classroom transform into a contortionist in attempts to stabilize her hoop.

portability. The hoop is exceptionally well designed. It pulls on the grainlines of the quilt only. The corners are rounded and gapped to leave the bias loose and unstretched. For the first time in the history of our industry, hand quilters have a hoop that won't warp their quilts during the stitching process!

Lap Hoops

There is a huge variety of hoops that fit into this category, ranging from plain round hoops to hoops mounted on a base that the quilter sits on for stability. The materials each is made from are equally varied. Further complicating these variables is the fact that each quilter has a unique body. Factors such as the length of torso, arm length, and the chair you sit on to quilt can spell the difference between the hoop working well for you or just getting in your way. One common characteristic of successful hoops, however, is weight. The heavier your hoop, the easier you will achieve That Perfect Stitch. This is because the hoop will counterbalance the pressure needed from the underneath hand. In most cases, the only way to achieve the kind of weight needed is to add a base to the hoop.

Round Hoops

Most wooden hoops are about the same. Some are prettier than others, and they vary in diameter. More information on hoop sizes is provided on page 85. Hoops have become increasingly lighter weight in the last decade, making them almost useless for fine hand quilting. If you can find an older one that is made from quality heavy woods like cherry wood, maple, or oak, it will serve you better and be a collectible at the same time.

There is a fiberglass hoop on the market that incorporates the ancient tongue-and-groove configuration. This is the No-Slip hoop by Morgan Hoops & Frames, in which a ridge on one hoop fits snugly into a groove on a second hoop as it is tightened. Although the hoop is thin, it is heavier than most newer wood hoops available, due to the fiberglass composite. One disadvantage of this hoop's unique tongue-and-groove feature, however, is evident during installation of the quilt. This hoop will not allow for adjustments once the quilt is placed in the hoop. If the quilter notices a slight distortion or problem area in the quilt after it is installed, there is no way to adjust tension in the hoop. The quilter has no choice but to quilt right over the problem spot.

Square and Oval Hoops

While square hoops and oval hoops may be pretty to look at, they do not offer any other advantages or disadvantages over round hoops. The only exceptions are the Grace Hoop2 (see page 84) and PVC plastic hoops. The square PVC plastic hoop is the single most portable hoop on the market. It pulls apart into small pieces that can be thrown into a quilt bag and off you go! It is also a heavy lap hoop due to the materials it is made from. The quilt is held in place with matching white plastic clamps that slide over the quilt on the straight edges only and press the quilt to the PVC pole. I have watched hundreds of women install quilts into this hoop and found almost every single one warped the quilt to varying degrees because all four sides are adjustable independently. It is very difficult to get the right tension in the quilt and adjust all the sides equally. This hoop also has distinct corners to its square-ness and, as you turn the hoop in your lap to quilt in your favorite direction, it is impossible to avoid poking yourself in the tummy with a corner. We've also discovered over the years that you shouldn't leave the quilt overnight in this particular hoop because the plastic clamps stretch out and eventually don't hold the quilt tightly enough. The hoop also doesn't fare well in the trunk of your car on a hot summer's day!

Lap Stands

Adding weight to lap hoops is an enormous advantage, so many of them are available on lap stands. As noted before, make sure that there is enough room between the hoop base and the hoop for your underneath hand to maneuver comfortably during quilting. Note, though, that it's possible for there to be too much room. If the hoop is set too high above the base, you will find that your shoulders are forced to rise up to accommodate it. If you can't relax your shoulders then everything else will be out of position, right down to your wrist, causing discomfort and affecting your stitch. If you happen to have a very long torso, then you can deal with tall lap stands. Most of us don't, and we need no more than about 4 to 6 inches (12 cm to 15 cm) from the base to the hoop. Although ball joints are a critical feature to a floor stand, they are an unnecessary added expense to a lap hoop. Further, they frequently require more space between the base and hoop, making them too tall for the average quilter's body. It is just as easy to turn the whole hoop in your lap. My favorite hoop is the Grace Hoop NonSwivel Lap Hoop. It weighs almost 5 pounds (2.25 kg) and is completely portable so I can use it on airplanes! The same hoop is available with the ball joint but is significantly taller in the lap and more expensive.

Tahitian Applique (incomplete), Dierdra A. McElroy.
*Shown in the Grace Hoop2 from Grace Company, this little quilt combines
straight-line quilting, crosshatch, and curves inside a colorful appliqué border*

Hoop Size

I have had the great privilege of visiting hundreds of personal sewing rooms over the last two decades. Whenever I visit a quilter's home, I get ideas on how to store fabric and organize my own things more efficiently. I can't help but laugh each time I see a row of nails across a wall with over a half dozen hoops hung on them. The idea that one should match the size hoop to the size of quilt being worked on is pervasive. When I first began doing research for my mother over 20 years ago, I challenged that concept and was met with much disapproval from her quilting bee friends. I am thrilled to see that today, many authors and instructors now agree. The human forearm is only so long! It doesn't matter if you are working on a king size quilt or a small placemat. That Perfect Stitch can only be achieved when you relax and stop contorting your body to make up for the shortfalls of products you are using.

I have elicited much laughter and teasing by asking quilters at guild meetings and other venues to let me measure their forearms. Surprisingly, the adult forearm does not seem to vary by more than three inches, regardless of height and bone structure. To measure yourself for a hoop, set the hoop on the inner bend of your elbow and see if your fingertips can touch the other side of the hoop at its longest diameter. Alternatively, use a tape measure to measure from the inner bend of your elbow to your fingertips, then round down to the nearest hoop size. For example, if the distance is 15 " (38 cm), then a 14 " (35 cm) hoop would be best. After teaching tens of thousands of students over the years I can tell you that a 14" (35 cm) hoop is the most functional for the average person. Yes, you might have slightly longer arms and can handle a 16" (40 cm) hoop or slightly shorter arms that best suit a 12" (30 cm) hoop. For the vast majority, though, the 14" (35 cm) hoop works best.

As we have seen, a hoop that is too big causes you to stretch out of position and round your shoulders uncomfortably, making it harder for you to control your stitches. If the hoop is on a stand, it might be top-heavy, too. A hoop that is too small can dramatically limit the quilting space available. Smaller hoops are lighter weight and cause control issues. Remember, it is best to avoid quilting within 2" (5 cm) of your hoop. This is because the hoop begins to interfere with wrist motions; the quilt won't warp the way it should, resulting in larger stitches that you have to work harder to achieve.

Placing the Quilt in a Hoop

The danger of quilting a large quilt in a hoop is the risk of distorting it. I am sure you have seen, more times than you care to remember, quilts on which the bottom edges are rippled or wavy, or where one side is shorter than the other. That distortion can occur all too easily if a quilter doesn't baste properly, isn't careful with the hoop while quilting, or doesn't use a hoop or frame at all!

You see, the most wonderful thing about fabric is its stretchability and the most awful thing about fabric is . . . its stretchability. Piecers love the straight of the grain and curse the bias. Appliquérs adore the bias and have to be very careful when working with the straight of the grain. A hand quilter must beware of the bias, not because it is difficult to quilt on, but because it is so easy to inadvertently distort your quilt in the hoop by pulling on the bias while adjusting it. Distortions are quilted in and the quilt will not relax back to its original shape. Since some of today's fabrics do not have a square thread count, I warn all my students against pulling on the quilt to adjust it. Instead, follow these guidelines on installing the quilt, and you will not run into distortion problems.

1. Make sure your quilt is basted densely enough to avoid distortions. Run basting lines from the center out to each edge, then run more basting lines from the center to each corner. Depending on the size of the quilt, keep running basting lines from the center outwards until no more than 3" (8 cm) is left unbasted between the radiating lines at the outer edge of the quilt. (See also page 74.)

2. Separate the two pieces of the hoop and place the inner hoop on a table. Center your quilt over the inner hoop. Place the outer hoop down over the quilt and the inner hoop. You may have to loosen the wing-nut of the hoop to accomplish this if you have a thick batting in your quilt. Tighten the outer hoop against the inner hoop until they are snug but not rock tight. They should be able to shift against each other but not easily. (If you are using the No-Slip Hoop, this step is especially important or Step 5 will be near impossible.) If you are using the Grace Hoop, skip to Step 4.

3. Tightening a hoop with a quilt in it can distort the quilt, depending on how much tightening you have to do. Most quilters pull on the edges of the quilt, but this serves only to distort the quilt even more. Instead, force the quilt hoop apart without loosening the wing-nut or other tightening mechanism. The quilt

will "spring" back to square the minute it is released from the hoop. Put the outer hoop back onto the quilt and inner hoop without tightening or loosening it, as it should be perfectly adjusted for the current quilt from Step 2. The quilt is now in the hoop and perfectly square!

4. Flip the hoop over and verify that no quilt corners got wrapped around the hoop and tucked up into it. Ignore all wrinkles and puckers; *do not* be tempted to pull on the quilt to remove them. The only things you should be concerned about here will be blatantly obvious to the eye, such as fabric caught up in folds or corners wrapped around hoops. If problems like this happen, go back to Step 3.

5. The quilt should now be smooth and flat, sitting beautifully inside the hoop. While this may look picture-perfect, the quilt is not yet ready to be quilted. Most likely, it is too taut in the hoop, making it extremely hard to warp the layers around the tip of the needle to achieve That Perfect Stitch. Spread your fingers apart as far as they will go and press in the center of the quilt. This should give your quilt a nicely concave look that means it is ready for stitching!

If you are using a PVC plastic hoop, here is how to install the quilt to avoid as much distortion as possible.

1. Assemble all the parts of the hoop and remove the clamps.
2. Center your quilt over the hoop squarely, meaning grain lines should run parallel to the side of your hoop. In most cases, this step is intuitive.
3. Snap all four clamps onto the poles
4. Rotate each clamp back up until it faces to the bottom towards your lap
5. Slowly rotate each clamp, one by one, until the first edge is lined up with the center of the pole. This step gives you a measurable way to know that you have adjusted each side the same and yet, since it drags the quilt with it, puts the right amount of looseness into the quilt for necessary tension.

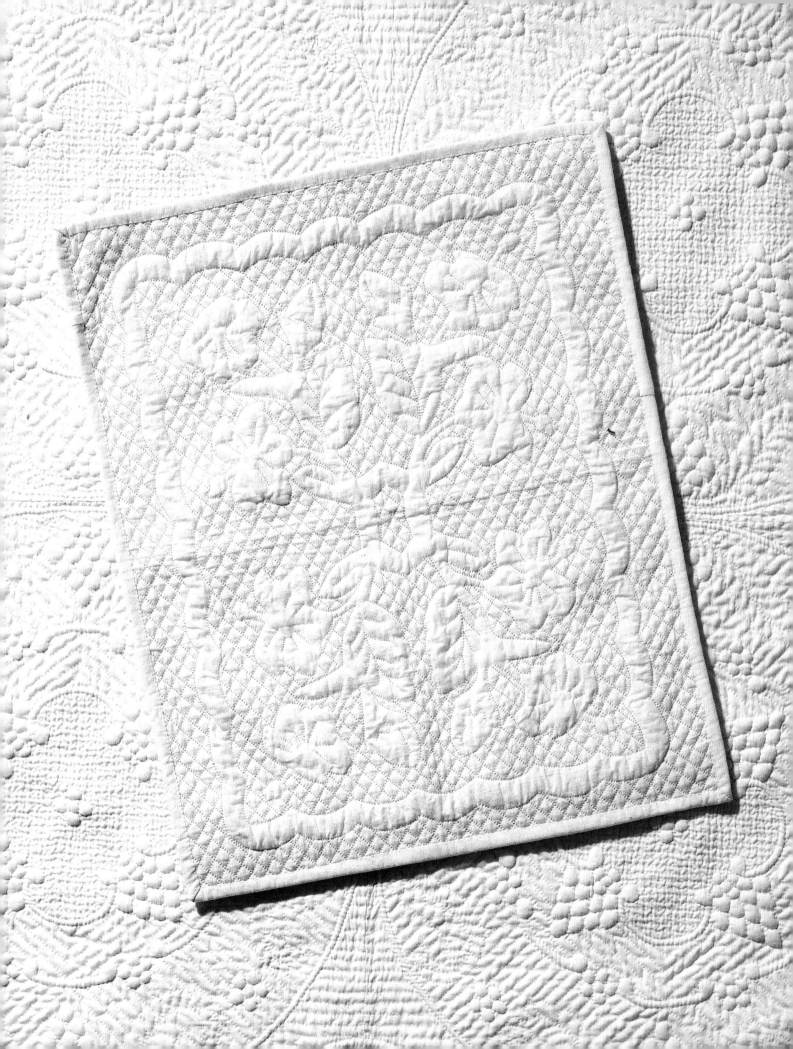

CHAPTER SEVEN

Markers

When I had been a quilter for several years, my great-aunt called me to tell me that we have a family heirloom quilt. It was made in 1930 by my great-grandmother and my great-aunts. Until that day, I had not been aware that anyone in my family had ever quilted! My great-aunt told us that she would send the quilt to me—to clean it for her. We decided that if this quilt had been kept that big a secret, we should accept the offer or we might never get to see it. When the box arrived, my mother carefully opened it. Tears came to her eyes when she saw what had happened. The lines of the quilting design had been marked onto the quilt top with the newest writing utensil to come to my great-grandmother's tiny Kansas farming community: ball-point pen. The lines were as bright a blue as the day they were marked.

Tahitian Hibiscus. Made by Roxanne McElroy.
*With a simple crosshatch design, this miniature whole-cloth quilt demonstrates that, with practice, the stitches on the top and on the back and the spaces on the top and on the back can be exactly the same length. It is shown on top of a wonderful white-on-white quilt, **Circles**, by Hazel Canny.*

Springtime over Baltimore. Made by Anita Askins.
*The white satin flowers are made from scraps left over from making a
wedding dress, which the quilter sewed for her daughter. This fabric is
reminiscent of the white silk used in antique album quilts.*

Choosing Markers

This sad story serves to show that what most of us would think is the easiest item to select for quilting has proven to be the toughest. The lesson to be learned is that *any* marking utensil should be tested. Just because it is new on the market and even if it claims to be designed for quilting, don't take chances with any marking utensil until you know for sure it will not damage your quilt. I've even seen incidences where a trusted marking tool that had been used by a quilter without incident for many years suddenly had issues. It may appear to be without reason, but think about the chemicals that might have been left in the fabrics by changing detergents, using fabric softeners, or applying spray sizing for ironing. Any number of those products could react with a marker causing it to be locked in permanently.

Markers are used to transfer the lines of a quilting design onto a quilt top so that it can be quilted. The goal is to find a marker that transfers onto the top with little effort, will stay on until all the quilting is done, and comes off afterward without leaving any chemicals or residue behind to damage the fibers of the quilt. It is important to test *all* marking tools for removability on *all* fabrics in the quilt top *before* the top is marked. This is the only way to assure yourself your quilt will be safe.

Pens

There is a type of marking pen on the market that I feel compelled to warn quilters against. There are several brand versions, but quilters know the pen as the "purple pen that vanishes." I had the pen analyzed by a chemist. The base chemical in this type of pen erodes the fibers of fabric, and, even though the color may disappear right away, the chemical is still there. My analyst also indicated that purple seems to be the only color that adheres to that particular chemical. It seems the color of the pen was chosen for this reason, not, as its marketers tout, for its ability to be seen on a wide range of fabrics.

Marker Test

I examined several different types of markers and evaluated them in terms of ease of movement over fabric, washability, and flexibility in marking a variety of colors and prints. On a scale of 1 to 10 (1 is poor, 10 is excellent), I assigned a rating to each. Here are my results.

Berol silver/white chalk	9
Roxanne's Quilter's Choice	10
Soapstone marker	7
Blue pens that wash out	2
Purple pens that vanish	1
#2 pencils	2
Ultimate marking pencil	4
Chalk pouncers	5
Hera marker	2

All ratings are based on my personal examinations of products I have used

One day I was visiting a quilt shop in Texas when an hysterical woman came into the shop with a bundle in her arms—a quilt she had finished two years before. She held part of the quilt between her hands with a line of quilting between her thumbs and gently pulled. The quilt top fabric tore away along the quilting stitches as if the fabric were a piece of perforated paper. The chemicals in "the purple pen that vanishes" had actually eaten the fabric along the lines where it was originally marked.

Another commonly used marker is known as the "blue pen that washes out." The manufacturer claims that the blue marks will stay on the fabric until removed with a damp sponge. My chemist told me the chemicals in this pen are very strong and the only color that can adhere to them is blue. Wiping with a damp sponge is not enough to rid the quilt of the blue color. If not actually soaked in water with a true soap for some time, the blue color tends to sink down through the quilt top and into the batting. It has a tendency to resurface again and again.

Even if the blue color does go, this does not mean the chemicals are gone as well. There are instances, not always, but enough times to raise concerns, where the chemicals have come back permanently as a dirty brown line. I've been told that the company response has been that the quilter had the quilt dry cleaned or ironed the quilt top after marking the quilting lines. Even if this is so, I could never recommend a pen with chemicals that so dramatically shorten the life of a quilt. There are just too many variables and chemical reactions possible that could destroy all of your hard work!

Soap and Chalk

Soap slivers used to be a good way to mark a quilt as they produced visible lines that would wash out later, right? The trouble with this is that today's manufactured soaps are not the same as those our grandmothers used.

Today, soaps have perfumes, moisturizers, dyes, and other chemicals in them. When you mark a quilt with a soap sliver you are essentially laying a concentrated line of chemicals down on the fabric through which your thread is going to run. One of the most frequent repercussions of this method has been faded fabric or thread where the soap sat for months.

Chalk is still the only material I trust for my quilts. Chalk markers come in a variety of delivery methods. A "bean bag" pouncer-type system works nicely if you are using templates to mark your design. The little fabric bag lets chalk dust come through and settle into the holes of the plastic template and onto your quilt top. Since this is a loose powder chalk, it will rub off the quilt very quickly. Most quilters find they can only mark a little as they go.

Another chalk comes in a plastic tube (similar to a lipstick) with a tiny metal wheel that clicks as you roll it across your fabric. This system lays a line of powdered chalk down on your quilt. This tool is good for marking straight lines and gentle curves, but I've found it difficult to mark intricate designs with it. The chalk is powdered and will rub off quickly, so marking very far ahead of yourself is impossible.

Tailors and seamstresses have traditionally used a chalk that is pressed into a hard flat cake with fine edges. It has worked its way into the hands of many a quilter and, while the marks stay on the fabric longer than powdered chalks, that is only because the chalk is pressed into wax which makes it stick longer to the quilt. Paraffin wax and beeswax are the only waxes that are truly safe and removable from fabric. Since the manufacturers do not divulge what types of wax are used in these markers, I don't trust them with my hand-made quilts.

One of the newer chalking methods is a powdered chalk that is put into what looks like a blackboard eraser. The manufacturer claims removal is as simple as either ironing or spraying with water. The application of heat to remove marks had me very concerned, so I poured a quarter inch pile of powder between two layers of fabric and ironed it. It became apparent immediately that there is wax in this system, as my fabric had a wet, oily spot that had soaked through. My conclusion was that while ironing may make the marks disappear, it did not remove the product.

I find chalk pencils to be the most trustworthy and flexible marker for quilting. The most intricate of designs can be created with them and the marks last longer than those made with powdered chalk. It is rare that I hear of chalk pencil not washing out of a quilt. The biggest complaint I hear from quilters about chalk pencils is the crumbling that can occur during sharpening. Chalk is brittle and cracks easily. The chalk is encased

Do Not Tap Pencils!

If you tap a pencil against a table it breaks the lead inside the wood and you will never get it sharpened. That is why using pencils as drumsticks is not a good idea. This is especially true with delicate chalk pencils. Simply dropping it onto your sewing table can cause the core lead to break.

in wood when bought in pencil format. If the pencil is banged harshly or dropped on a hard floor, the chalk shatters. It won't be readily apparent, since the wood casing hides the damage. Yet when you try to sharpen a damaged pencil, you'll find you waste half the pencil before getting a sharp point. There is no way to repair a damaged pencil. Luckily, they are relatively inexpensive and can be easily replaced. Treat them gently instead of throwing them in a drawer with other tools or letting them roll off your design table onto the floor. I find that electric sharpeners, those that require the pencil to be inserted straight up and down versus sideways, are much less harsh on the pencil during sharpening. Avoid hand-crank wall sharpeners, as well as costly designer eye-brow pencil sharpeners.

One last word of caution, chalk pencils are only safe in their two naturally occurring colors—gray/silver and white. Beware of pencils that are yellow, red, blue, or green. These pencils have added dyes and may not wash out successfully

Pencils

The most basic marking tool is, of course, the common pencil. The graphite in pencils, commonly referred to as the lead, comes in many different hardnesses. The softer the graphite, the more residue rubs off onto the fabric fibers. Harder graphites are more difficult to see on fabric since they leave less residue, and, as a result, quilters tend to press much harder with them, forcing the graphite into the fibers. When this happens, it becomes even more difficult than softer graphite to get out of the fabric. Graphite is particularly problematic on painted fabric. More and more we are seeing quilts in which the graphite has not washed out of the painted parts of the fabric.

Many otherwise perfect quilts have lead pencil marks that remain to detract from their beauty. The appraised value of a quilt is affected by these marks and new quilts in competition are eliminated if the marks show.

I found a pencil that surpasses anything my mother and I have yet used. As a matter of fact, we liked the pencil so much that I bought the company that makes it. That way, I would be assured an unending supply. The pencil, Quilter's Choice, comes in silver or white. It is a little softer than Berol so it marks with a little less force. It also needs to be sharpened less and holds a point very well, as it has an organic compound that stops excessive crumbling. Quilter's Choice is photographed at the beginning of this chapter. It is now available from Colonial Needle Co.

Alternative Marking Methods

Naturally, quilters have sought out marking methods that don't require putting pen, pencil, or chalk marks on their quilts. Quilters have used sticky papers and masking tape, for instance, to quilt in straight lines. The goal is to find something that will stay stuck while manipulating the quilt during stitching without leaving residues that will attract dirt or create dark shadows later on. Blue painter's tape, available at hardware store, achieves those goals more successfully than masking tape.

The best product I have seen is Stick N Stitch. Unfortunately, it is no longer available, but I keep hoping it makes a comeback. Stick N Stitch was made of a tissue-thin but very strong material, with the equivalent of a freezer paper backing that stabilized it. Stick N Stitches came in every shape imaginable, from hearts to intricately curved feathers. To use, the quilter just peeled off the backing, stuck the shape to the quilt, and stitched around the edges. To make it easier for quilt shops to carry the product, Stick N Stitch was also sold in 81/2" x 11" sheets that could be run through a computer printer. Hundreds of designs, all size-adjustable, were available on CD. The shape was then cut out by hand and used on the quilt. These pieces could be repositioned about a dozen times before losing their stickiness. Best of all, they left no sticky residues behind!

Quilter's Workshop

1. Choose a variety of fabrics and marking utensils. Mark each fabric with each marker. Allow to sit for a period of time and then wash. Note the marker, the method of washing, and the type of soap on the back of each piece of fabric in permanent ink. Observe the marks on each fabric and draw conclusions based on the marker and type of fabric.

2. Repeat the exercise above, but this time subject fabrics to different conditions before washing. Be sure to note the types of conditions tested on the back of each piece of fabric. Test the effects of ironing, storage under fluorescent lights, storage in a dark closet, and erasing markings with a soft eraser.

CHAPTER EIGHT

Other Helpful Aids

O ver the years, quilters have used the most unexpected tools to help them with their quilting. We are lucky that today there are products on the market for virtually every need we may have. There are still a few unconventional items, however, that at first seem out of place in a sewing kit, but that no serious quilter would be without. Necessity is the mother of invention. I encourage you as a quilter to invent when necessary. All too often quilters blame their lack of expertise or dexterity for any problems they encounter while hand quilting. When you run into a problem, ask "why" first. Analyze the collection of products you are using in the quilt to determine what is going wrong. Then find a way to fix it. No rights or wrongs if it works for you!

Hedge Rose. Made by Martha A. Nordstrand.
Hand applique, hand embroidery and hand embellishment with a freehand all-over quilting design.

Orangutan. Made by Nancy S. Brown, Outland, CA.

Background quilting is done in a crazy quilt pattern. Most of the other quilting follows the natural lines of the orangutan, leaves, and trees.

Protecting Your Fingers

Once you have mastered That Perfect Stitch, you will have no sore fingers at all. However, while you are learning to coordinate your movements, you will sometimes get them out of sequence and will end up with a few needle pricks on your fingers. Generally, I do not recommend using anything to protect your fingers on the hand underneath the quilt because it is imperative to feel the needle in order to stop pushing in time. A few quilters have fingers so sensitive that they need to use something, however. Aunt Becky's is a metal tool bent into a tent shape. With practice, you can learn to manipulate it under the quilt. The down side is that you must be somewhat ambidextrous in order to coordinate both hands, the tool, and the needle all at once. Another issue is that the quilting needle tends to dull quickly due to contact with the metal tool.

Within a couple of days of beginning to quilt, a callus should form to help protect your finger. This callus should not be achieved through painful stabs or by leaving blood stains on the back of the quilt. It forms as the skin's natural reaction to abrasion. While the callus forms, there is a product in almost all drug stores that will help a little. New Skin or Skin Shield comes in liquid form or a convenient spray. A couple of coats on the underneath finger will provide a thin protective coating between your finger and the needle point. Be absolutely certain the product is dry before touching your quilt, however, because it does contain a strong chemical. Once dry, it just peels or washes off.

You can also buy tape specifically designed to protect the fingers from needle pricks. I hesitate to use any kind of tape, however, that will be near my needle point because tape residue always adheres to the needle and a build-up causes drag. Additionally, muting the feeling of the underneath finger often hinders a quilter from learning when to push and when to stop pushing. Frequently, protective tapes are not strong enough to withstand the tiny needle point and end up being sewn to the back of the quilt! For that reason, little metal disks that stick to the pad of your finger were designed, but they dull the needle and actually cause a lack of control because of their convex shape. The needle tip hits the disk and slides right off, causing you to lose your stitch *and* poke your finger!

In my classrooms, if a quilter needs protection for her fingers I pass out an inexpensive product called Thimble-Its. These are clear plastic oval discs that stick to the finger. They are hard enough to protect the finger yet not soft enough to get sewn to the back of the quilt easily. They are not puncture proof, as they are thin enough to allow you to feel the needle.

Sore Fingers

If you are on a deadline and your finger is getting too sore to sew, I have a sure overnight cure: Preparation H. As well as softener and antiseptic, it contains a mild analgesic for pain.

Taking Care of the Quilter's Callus

It is very important to gain a callus to help protect your finger. Take care, however, that the callus does not thicken to the point that it is impossible to feel the needle coming through the layers of the quilt. Use an emery board to file down the callus to a manageable thickness.

If you are considering using a cream on your callused finger, be sure you choose the correct one for the problem. Bag Balm is popular, and you can find it at most quilt shops. It is also available from feed supply stores—a can will last you and few hundred of your closest friends for life! Designed to soften the udders of cows and prevent infection when nursing, Bag Balm is somewhat greasy. A less greasy version is Udder Cream. Both contain softeners and antiseptics. They do nothing for the pain if your finger is sore. Both of these are pH balanced for cows rather than for people, and they do not absorb easily into the skin.

Preparation H is a more suitable product. It is pH balanced for human skin, it contains softeners, and it has mild analgesics for relief of soreness. The cream version applied to sore callused fingers at night has measurable effects by morning. I do, however, suggest that you transfer the product to a cuter container than the one it is sold in if you will be carrying it in your sewing kit to the quilting bee!

I cannot recommend strongly enough that every quilter purchase a paraffin bath, available from department stores and drug stores. Slather your hands heavily in an aloe vera-based hand cream, then quickly dip them into the bath. Let the first layer dry and repeat until you have ten layers on each hand. Enlist the help of a family member to wrap plastic bags around your hands. Sit and relax until the wax is cold. This process provides a therapeutic, deep-

Scottish Thistle. Made by Roxanne McElroy.

Quilting along the dividing lines of plaid fabric can give the illusion of a pieced background.

Threading Tip

One of my friends has somehow gotten her grandkids all excited about threading needles for her. Whenever the grandkids visit she has them thread 50 needles onto a spool of thread. Then she just pulls one needle and a length of thread away from the spool, keeping all the other needles down at the spool, and off she goes!

moisturized heat penetration to the joints of your hand, as well as, moisturizing skin and softening calluses. It can be done as many times per day as you choose and provides significant relief for arthritic joints. Try your feet as well!

Protecting Your Eyes

I urge you to see your ophthalmologist before you get heavily into quilting. Most doctors automatically make you a prescription for a reading distance of 18″ (46 cm). We can easily move a book to the right distance to read, but that is not the case with quilting. Take your quilting with you to the doctor and demonstrate how you sit to quilt. Your doctor will gladly make a prescription right for you.

If you cannot thread a needle in a couple of tries, then I suggest you use a needle threader. Why waste your eyes on something as simple as that when you will need your expert eyesight to see the tiny stitches you will be making? There are a phenomenal amount of needle threaders on the market, including one that sits on the table top and loads thread into your needle at the push of a button. It can be rather finicky about types of needles but many quilters swear by it. I prefer one that takes up less room in my sewing bag and looks much like a tiny credit card with a thin metal wand on the end.

Aids for Faster Quilting

Once we find our special rhythm, it is upsetting to stop and pull the needle through all the fine stitches stacked on the needle. Sometimes we hate so much to stop that we find we have put so many stitches on the needle that we can no longer pull it through at all. Other times, our fingers feel so tired or weak we can barely pull two to three stitches through smoothly. In these situations, we need a product that will grab the needle and pull it through for us, without slowing us down or damaging the needle. At quilt shops you can buy Needle Grabbits, rubber discs the size of a fifty cent piece, and they are quite effective. If you have a friend who is a nurse, rubber tourniquets work quite well, too. The only downside to Needle Grabbits and similar products is that they slow you down slightly, since you have to let go of your needle, pick up the product, pull the needle through, then drop the product again before you can reposition for the next run of stitches. This small loss of time is well worth it if you have any hand challenges such as carpal tunnel syndrome or arthritis. The pain of repetitive pinching and the force required for fine hand quilting stitches can be intolerable, after all.

Another popular item to use is the finger cot, available at most drug stores and quilt shops. Roll it over and down your finger to help get a good grip on the needle to pull it through the layers. The finger cot is especially helpful for quilters with hand challenges. It is a great time-saver, since there is no picking up and putting down to do. The rubber is very thin and can be rolled further down the finger or just over the tip, depending on your comfort level. A finger cot is reusable if you remove it carefully by re-rolling it up the finger and storing it in your sewing kit. Latex-free finger cots are not nearly as effective at gripping the needle, since rubber is not sticky. If you have small fingers, you can buy penny balloons and snip the tops off. They are less expensive than finger cots and come in pretty colors!

Thread Care Aids

For a variety of reasons, you may end up having to use a quilting thread that is not optimally constructed for hand work. The fraying and knotting that can result from using a sub-par thread can drive you batty! If the color of that thread is critical to the aesthetic design of your quilt and yet it is constantly knotting up and you feel like it will be ten years before you could possibly finish, then try waxing the thread. This will seal the tiny hairs that are grabbing one another and give some abrasion protection as the thread is dragged through the quilt. You can purchase beeswax or paraffin wax in cute shapes at quilt shops or craft stores. Although just pulling a length of thread through the wax will afford some protection, more than likely, most of the wax will rub off into your quilt after the first pull or two. For best results, run the thread through the wax and then heat-set the wax into the thread by either ironing or setting it in the oven on cookie sheets lined with parchment paper. If I know I am going to have to do this, I prepare fifty lengths of thread at a time.

There is a product on the market that quilters are tempted to buy but that my research warns against. Thread Heaven comes in an adorable blue box. The product inside is opaque and sparkly. It is marketed as a thread conditioner. In my tests, I have found it to be completely ineffectual. It will not help you thread your needle or prevent knots.

Don't Use Forceps!

Some quilters use forceps to grab the needle. I cannot recommend this practice even if the forceps are rubber tipped. Although the rubber will prevent the stripping of the metal plating from your needle, there is still a risk of pulling at an angle and bending the needle. The wear and tear on the hand from grabbing and squeezing the tool is also not good in the long run.

CHAPTER NINE

The Quilting Stitch

As you will find out, the quilting stitch is quite intricate, involving a sequence of precise finger movements. For a lucky few, it takes just a few minutes to learn. For others, it feels awkward and takes a few hours' practice. But when you get it right, it is like being hit by a thunderbolt. Perfect stitches soon become second nature—nothing looks or feels better. Nothing, that is, except the sheer joy of completing your own beautiful handmade quilt. Hand quilting, when done properly, is relaxing, soothing, and satisfying. There should be no pain in the arm, hand, or shoulder or underneath your fingers. Once you master That Perfect Stitch, you will create amazing works of art.

Circles. Made by Hazel Canny.
This incredible white-on-white quilt demonstrates exquisite stitches in a trapunto design. The quilt above is **Hummingbirds,** *made by Dierdra McElroy.*

For That Perfect Stitch, the stitches on the back of the quilt should be as close as possible in size to those on the front. This takes practice, but it is not impossible. On some of my best quilts, the stitches on the back are identical in size to the stitches on the front. On Tahitian Hibiscus (see page 88), for example, the front and the back are indistinguishable. You can tell if your quilting is even if the stitches on the front and back of the quilt and the spaces on the front and back of the quilt are exactly the same length.

Threading the Needle

If you look at a piece of thread through a strong magnifying glass or a microscope, you will clearly see the *knap*, its featherlike surface (see page 49). Every time thread is pulled through fabric, the knap wears a little thinner and the thread gradually weakens. To minimize this, cut thread to a length of no more than 18″ (46 cm). This also helps avoid tangles when quilting. Better yet, use Gutermann or YLI hand-quilting thread because they have no knap at all.

If you are using a thread with a knap, such as Metler by Metrosene, make sure you pull the thread through the fabric in the right direction. Pulling against the knap is like pulling a feather through a tiny hole against its natural grain. How can you tell which way the knap lies? Since knap is a result of the way in which thread was wrapped onto the spool in the factory, the answer is easy: simply remember always to knot the end of the thread that comes off the spool *last*! If you are planning several hours of quilting at one time, it is a good idea to thread 10 or even 20 needles before you begin. Without cutting, thread them all onto the end of the thread of a single spool. Separate the first needle from the rest by unreeling about 18″ (46 cm) of thread, cut, and knot. Leave the rest of the needles on the spool until you are ready to use them. An added bonus is that all your needles are threaded while your eyes are fresh!

Making the Quilter's Knot

1. Take the threaded needle in the fingers of the dominant hand so that the thread hangs down.

2. With the other hand, draw the tail of the thread up toward the eye of the needle. The tail of the thread meets the tip of the needle head-on.

3. Close the circle by completely, overlapping the needle so that the very end of the tail presses against the eye of the needle.

4. Hold the tail against the needle with one hand.

5. With the other hand, wrap the thread around the point three times in any direction.

6. Push the wraps down toward the eye and hold them down with the index finger and thumb of the dominant hand to keep them from unwinding.

7. With the other hand, grab the point of the needle. Do not let go of the needle and wrapped thread.

Making the Quilter's Knot

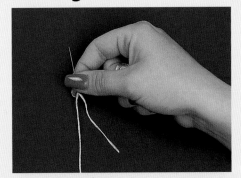
1. Let thread hang down.

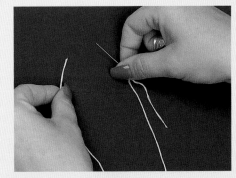
2. Tail meets tip of needle.

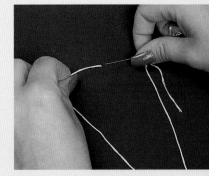
3. Close the circle.

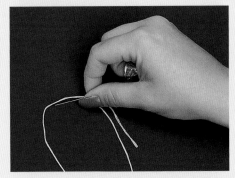
4. Hold tail against needle.

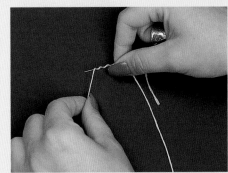
5. Wrap thread three times.

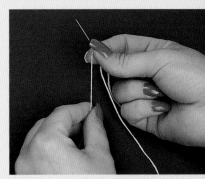
6. Push wraps down and hold.

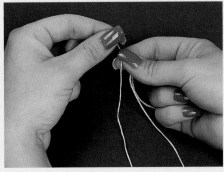
7. Grab point of needle.

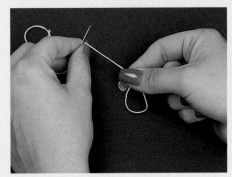
8. Pull threaded needle up and out.

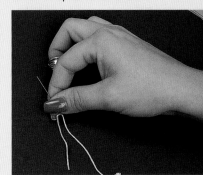
9. A neat knot forms.

8. While still pinching the wraps with the fingers of the dominant hand, pull the threaded needle up and out the full length of the thread.

9. By the time the end of the thread is reached, a neat consistently sized knot will form somewhere between ¼″ to ½″ (0.5 cm to 1 cm) from the end of the thread. Do not trim off the tail of the thread or the knot might manage to untie itself between the layers of the quilt. The size of the knot is important. If it is too small, it might pop out, and if it is too big, it might damage the weave of the fabric in the quilt top.

Beginning to Quilt

Always begin stitching in the middle of the quilt, not at the outer edges. This way, you avoid inadvertently locking ripples in the center. Also, as you work from the center out to the edges, it is much easier to keep all the layers smooth and aligned.

A quilt is never worked from the back, always from the front. To hide the knot, insert the needle about ¾″ (2 cm) from the point you wish to start quilting. Push the needle through the quilt top and the batting, but not through the backing. Skip the needle between the layers and bring the point up to the surface at the precise spot where you decided the quilting should begin. When the knot stops, gently pop it into the center of the quilt. Push the yarns of the fabric where the knot has passed back into position by running a fingernail over the surface of the quilt top.

One of my mother's quilts, *Wedding Rings and Champagne Bubbles on a Bed of Roses* (see page 32), came back from a national competition with only one criticism from a judge who stated, "When the quilt is held up to the light, the tails of the threads do not go in the right direction." I concluded the only way to keep this criticism from showing up again in the future would be to run the needle between the layers *along a line of quilting or along a line to be quilted.* That way, all the tails are camouflaged along the line! A hidden benefit turned out to be once in a while I actually quilted back over some of those tails and it reinforced my quilting!

Making the Stitch

Fast, efficient, and easy to learn, the quilting stitch, once mastered, results in small even stitches that turn a beautifully designed quilt into a fine piece of handwork. Because it causes virtually no stress on the hand or fingers, a quilter who uses the quilting stitch correctly can work quickly and for longer periods, with the last stitch as perfect as the first.

1. Balance the needle at a perpendicular 90° angle through the layers of the quilt between the middle finger of the top hand and the index finger of the bottom hand. No other part of the hand should touch the needle. Do not push on the needle yet; you will know if you do, because your bottom finger will hurt!

2. Without pushing on the needle, causing it to advance through the fabric, gently lay the needle backward, away from your body. The finger underneath pushes up forcefully to ensure that the needle

does not advance farther than it should. The tighter the fabric is around your needle, the less likely it is that the needle will slip through to the underneath fabric. Move the thumb into position on the quilt near the point at which the needle will resurface.

3. Lay the needle all the way back so that the tip is pointing up. Make sure the eye is at 12 o'clock and the point is at 6 o'clock. The thumb should be pushing down forcefully on the quilt top immediately in front of the needle tip. (I even dig grooves in the nail polish on my thumb to keep the needle from slipping.) The underneath finger continues to push the needle up so that it will resurface as quickly as possible. Only at this time, when the thumb has pushed *down* and the finger from below is pushing *up* hard, push on the needle and take the stitch. *Stop pushing* as soon as the needle tip is visible.

4. With the needle gently caught in a dimple on the thimble, gently *lift* it back up to a perpendicular angle so that it can barely be felt by the index finger below. This is strictly a rotational movement; the needle should not advance any farther through the fabric.

5. Once the needle is back up to the perpendicular position, you are ready to begin the second stitch. This is exactly the same position as Step 1, except there is now a stitch stacked on the needle.

6. The underneath finger can now stop pushing *up*, allowing the thimble finger to push the needle *down*. The underneath finger should be feeling for the needle tip to clear the fabric. As soon as you feel it, *stop pushing*!

7. Repeat Step 1 to Step 6 to stack a second, third, and fourth stitch on the needle. Pull the needle through the stack of stitches to the end of the thread and then give a gentle tug to tighten. Pull the thread through with the same tension with every stack of stitches to result in a consistent, even line of quilting.

8. The number of stitches you can stack varies with the size of your stitches. The general rule is when you can no longer pivot the needle back up to a full 90° angle, it is time to pull through. The needle may bend with stitches on it and you will definitely appear to warp the fabric, but the needle did rotate all the way up. Probably one more stitch and it will be time to pull through.

1. Correct

2. Incorrect

3. Incorrect

The Quilting Position

1. *Correct quilting position. Quilt toward your body whenever you have an option. Keep the shoulder down and relaxed, the elbows down, the wrist straight, and the fingers gently curved and relaxed.*

2. *Incorrect position. The raised shoulder causes the back to lean, the elbow tight against the side, the wrist bent backward, and the fingers stiff. This position causes pain and can lead to such conditions as arthritis, carpal tunnel syndrome, tendinitis, and headaches.*

3. *Also incorrect position. Keep shoulders and elbows down, but relaxed.*

Making the Stitch

1. Balance needle at 90° angle.

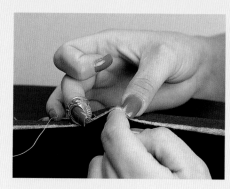

2. Lay needle backward.

3. Take stitch.

4. Lift needle back up.

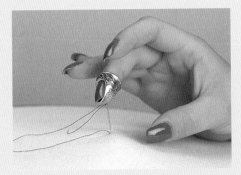

5. Back to 90° angle.

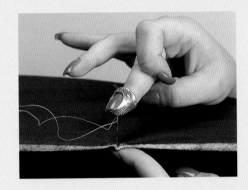

6. Feel for the needle tip.

7. Take second stitch.

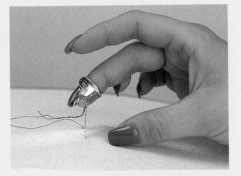

8. When you cannot return needle to 90° angle, pull through.

This sequence of photographs shows the precise positions of the top and bottom hands during the quilting stitch. Done correctly, the stitch causes no stress on the hands or fingers and results in small, even stitches.

Hiding the Knot

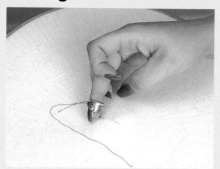

1. Poke needle through layers.

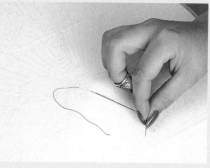

2. Pull on thread.

3. Pop knot between layers.

4. Pull taut and snip thread.

How to Stop Quilting

When the thread is down to about 6" (15 cm) long, it is time to knot-off. Loop the thread round in a circle. Bring the needle up through the circle. Hold the circle down with a finger while reducing its circumference by pulling on the threaded needle. The goal is to get the knot to form about ¼" (0.5 cm) from the quilt top. Poke the needle back through the same hole from which it exited the quilt, jump at least ½" (1 cm) between the layers, resurface, and "pop" the knot between the layers. Cut the thread close to the quilt top. After threading a new needle, jump through the layers and bring the needle back up through that same hole you made when you knotted off. This way, from the back of the quilt, it will not look as though you missed a stitch.

Stitches Per Inch

A perfect line of stitching is, most importantly, an even line of stitching. Even quilting is achieved when all the stitches and all the spaces between the stitches on the front and on the back of the quilt are exactly the same

How to Stop Quilting

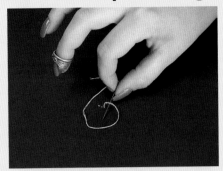

1. Loop thread around in a circle.

2. Bring needle up through circle.

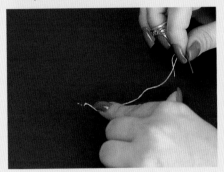

3. Pull on threaded needle to form knot.

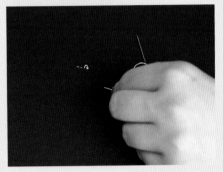

4. Jump needle between layers and pop knot.

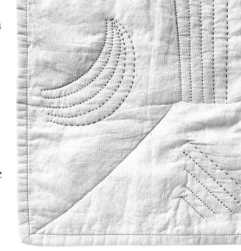

length. Just as you hear rhythm in music, you can *feel* rhythm in quilting. With practice, you can feel that the needle is in exactly the right place and can react at exactly the same instant with every stitch. As you rock back and forth, you know the momentum is steady and the stitches are perfectly spaced. Even stitches come from doing exactly the same thing every single time. As with any other skill, practice makes perfect! How many stitches are there per inch in a perfect line of quilting? The sample here shows lines of 8, 10, 12, 14, and 16 stitches per inch. Below is a simple gauge by which you can judge your progress.

6 stitches per inch = Accomplished   (2.5 stitches per cm = Accomplished)
8 stitches per inch = Average   (3 stitches per cm = Average)
10 stitches per inch = Expert   (4 stitches per cm = Expert)
12 stitches per inch = Professional   (5 stitches per cm = Professional)
14 stitches per inch = Micro Quilter   (5.5 stitches per cm = Micro Quilter)
16 stitches per inch = Weaver!   (6 stitches per cm = Weaver!)

Getting Off on the Wrong Foot

Unfortunately, many beginning quilters start off on the wrong foot by using a basic stitch that they have taught themselves or, worse still, have learned from others. Here are two common styles of hand sewing that will never result in That Perfect Stitch.

Stab Stitching

Stitch by stitch, the left hand "stabs" the needle at a perpendicular angle through the quilting layers, while the right hand waits underneath to grab it and pull it through. Once a little thread is through, the needle is turned around and poked back up through the layers, where the left hand is waiting to grab it and start the process again. After eight or ten stabs, the thread is pulled through. Besides being slow and cumbersome, stab stitching usually results in sloppy, uneven stitches, mainly because, when working from the underside, it is impossible for the quilter to see exactly where the stitches are going. This technique is aggravated still by quilters who use their dominant hand on top instead of below. More control is needed below, where the quilter does not have the advantage of sight.

Running Stitch

It is easy to look at a quilt and conclude that the quilting stitches resemble a simple line of running stitch. Beginner quilters, especially those who are self-taught, use the running stitch, holding the needle between the index finger and thumb and guiding it through the layers. Some use a thimble on the middle finger to help the needle along. While it is easy for novices to learn, the running stitch has its drawbacks. First, it is stressful on the joints of the fingers, because of the "pinching pressure" needed to guide the needle up and down through the layers. Second, it is very difficult to achieve small even stitches, especially when quilting through seam allowances. More than 10 stitches per inch (4 stitches per cm) is impossible, since the needle cannot be turned around in a short enough space to achieve a perpendicular angle on both the down-thrust and the up-thrust.

No matter how tiny you make your stitches, remember that *evenness*, not size, is the single most important element of quilting. Quilt appraisers prefer an even 8 stitches per inch (3 stitches per cm) to a sloppy 12 (5). If a quilter has gained enough control to produce even stitches, then it's much easier to increase the number of stitches per inch (cm). If you concentrate on making your stitches even rather than small, you will very soon develop a rhythm. Interestingly, my experience has been that the larger the stitches, the more difficult it is to make them straight and even. Try Workshop 1 below and you will see what I mean—it is very challenging, but it will teach you a lot about the quilting stitch.

There is another reason why size of stitches is not all-important. The stitches you make must be appropriate to the quilting design you are following. Obviously, the quilt design should match the theme of a quilt, and if bigger stitches are more suitable, so be it. I have even met fine quilters who simply do not like the look of 14 stitches per inch (5.5 stitches per cm). The point is, you must experiment to find That Perfect Stitch for you and for the quilt you are making.

Quilter's Workshop

1. Sandwich 180 (45 cm) squares of fabric, batting, and backing together. With a chalk marking pencil, draw five parallel lines on the fabric. With a very visible quilting thread, quilt along the first row, deliberately attempting just 6 even stitches per inch (2.5 stitches per cm). When you are finished, go on to the next row and quilt 8 stitches per inch (3 stitches per cm). Finish the next lines with 10, 12, and 14 stitches per inch (4, 5, and 5.5 stitches per cm). Remember that it will not be possible to make 14 stitches per inch (5.5 stitches per cm) unless you selected a fabric with a good thread count (see page 2) as well as a good hand-quilting batt (see page 12).

2. The easiest quilting job is whole cloth—a quilt made of unpieced fabric covered with intricate quilting stitches. Whole cloth is ideal for practicing the quilting stitch. There are no cumbersome seam allowances, and the fabric is the same all over, which means it is easy to develop a rhythm and make all the stitches even. Make a miniature whole-cloth quilt, mark a simple quilting design, and stitch.

CHAPTER TEN

Quilting Techniques

Once you have mastered That Perfect Stitch, you will find that you still have to adjust your technique slightly to handle various situations and directions required by different quilting designs. Even a nice quilting stitch can appear sloppy if made in unnatural directions. As mentioned in the previous chapter, quilting south is the most comfortable and orthopedically correct direction. At a frame you may not be able to turn your quilting line toward you, so adjust the angle you are sitting at to position the line correctly. Some cases require short periods of creative quilting, such as thumb quilting, in order to work away from yourself. In this chapter you will learn about these and other common situations a quilter will encounter.

Bottom to top: *Tricycles and Trains* (in drawer) by Roxanne McElroy; *Les Sirenes (The Mermaids)* by Roxanne McElroy; *Jewell's Paradise* by Roxanne McElroy; *Victorian Orchid* by Dierdra McElroy; *Scottish Thistle* by Roxanne McElroy; *Mermaids in the Surf* by Roxanne McElroy; *Ia Orana* by Dierdra McElroy; *Wedding Rings and Champagne Bubbles on a Bed of Roses* (hanging down) by Roxanne McElroy.

With the Grain

Ideally, we would all like always to be able to quilt diagonally across the grain of the fabric. Quilting parallel with the grain causes problems, because quilting thread is naturally inclined to "kiss up to" the nearest yarn of fabric running parallel with it, which makes some of the stitching disappear. This happens more frequently with thread that is not waxed, because the lighter weight matches the weight of the yarns in the fabric itself. Be careful, too with fabrics with a 60/60 thread count, because the yarns of these fabrics are actually heavier than the heaviest quilting thread!

Thumb Quilting

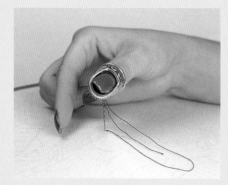

1. Balance needle at 90° angle.

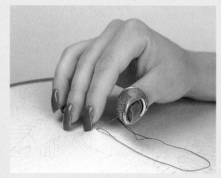

2. Lay needle down.

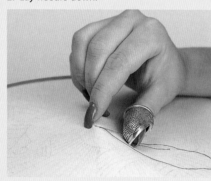
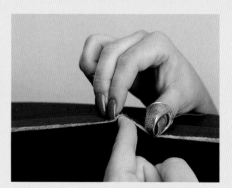

3. Take stitch.

The principle of thumb quilting is exactly the same as the normal quilting stitch, but the thumb and middle finger reverse roles. Work slowly and wear a thimble on your thumb to minimize pressure. The thumb rotates and pushes the needle, while the forefinger pushes the fabric down in front of the needle before it resurfaces.

Quilting in Straight Lines

Quilting *south*—or quilting toward you—is the easiest direction in which to quilt, simply because of the natural location of your thumb in relationship with your hand. It also allows for relaxed shoulders, elbows, and wrists so that you can quilt better for longer periods of time. It is a good idea, when quilting on a hoop, always to quilt south. On a full frame, however, this is not as easy, though a quilter soon learns to twist around on her chair in order to quilt toward her. There are times when you will need to quilt *north*—or away from you—for example, to avoid having to knot-off the thread and re-enter from the opposite direction. *Thumb quilting*, as it is called, takes practice, but means that you can quilt north for short lengths and still achieve That Perfect Stitch. Sometimes when thumb quilting, you may feel your stitches are not quite straight. When you pivot the needle back, make sure that it is lying along the quilting line before you push for the stitch. If you are a prolific quilter and use a full-size quilt frame, it may be wise to invest in a good thimble for your thumb. Otherwise, temporary fixes might be leather thimbles or a thimble that does not quite fit your thumb but that suffices for a few stitches.

Quilting Curves

The difficulty in quilting a tight curve lies in the fact that there is a limit to the number of stitches you are able to stack as you work around the curve. This means it is difficult to set and maintain an even rhythm while you quilt. No matter how tight the curve, never stack less than two stitches before pulling the thread through the quilt. If you quilt one stitch at a time, it is virtually impossible to maintain evenness of stitches and tension.

Quilting Through Seam Allowances

A common mistake when quilting through bulky seam allowances is to resort to stab stitching, which too often results in uneven and unattractive stitching lines. A simple method of backstitch allows you to maintain That Perfect Stitch. As you approach the seam allowance, instead of setting the needle in front of the point at which the thread emerged from layers, set it one stitch-length behind this point, cutting the length of the stitch space in half. Repeat, one stitch at a time, until you are through the seam allowance and can safely continue the speedier

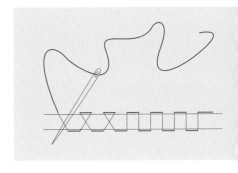

Topsy's Star. Made by Rheba Rozeboom.
The design in the corner squares and the setting triangles are made by using a corner stencil four times. The background quilting accents the feathers. The border feathers look like trapunto because of the amount of background quilting.

Star of the Blue Grass (detail).
Made by Elaine Rothermel, Oxnard, CA.
Trapunto with stippling around the ferns.

quilting stitch. If you have many seam allowances, switch to a needle one size larger so you can exert more pressure.

Jumping Lines

To avoid having to knot-off and re-enter at the end of each line of quilting, jump from one line to the next between the layers. Particularly if you are quilting with dark thread on a light fabric, be sure your needle also goes below the batting to keep the thread from shadowing through the top of the quilt. Jumping lines helps you quilt faster. It also means you have to tie fewer knots, giving you a stronger quilt.

Jumping Lines

Allow room for one last stitch.

Insert needle through top layer and batting only, not backing.

Resurface needle at position you wish to continue quilting.

Pull thread through taut.

Quilter's Workshop

1. Practice quilting on a curve by tracing four circles of different sizes onto a muslin top. Add batting and backing and put it into a hoop. Start with the largest circle. Quilting curves requires the quilter to take it a little slower. Make sure the tip of the needle resurfaces on the line. I cannot tell you how many stitches to take before pulling through, because it depends on the size of the stitches you are making. The general rule is that when you can no longer bring the needle back up to a 90° angle with all the stitches stacked on it, it is time to pull through. The smaller the circle, the fewer stitches you can take. Try always to do at least two stitches, though, for consistency. Now, move on to the next largest and note the differences between the two.

2. Pull out a quilt that has some seam allowances in it and practice quilting through them. If you do not have a quilt in progress, create a small pieced top by sewing strips together and adding batting and backing. Quilt horizontally across the strips to encounter as many seams as possible. Check the back frequently and compare it to the front. Using a size 9 Betweens will help, as will highly visible thread.

CHAPTER ELEVEN

Quilting Designs

Quilters spend considerable time designing their quilt tops. Once the overall design is chosen, the colors must be exactly right. Sometimes, the quilt top takes as much as a year to finish. Yet it never ceases to amaze me how frequently I hear, "Now I just have to quilt it and it will be done." It is as though the quilting is nothing more than a routine, hurry-and-get-through-it finishing process, one that cannot be ignored but that does not warrant much time. The truth is that even a quilt that has an award-winning design and brilliant color scheme will be reduced to mundane if it has an uninspired quilting design that is poorly executed. Although the quilt design is quilted over the patchwork or appliqué design, it *never* covers it up; it only adds to the quilt's overall look.

Wedding Rings and Champagne Bubbles on a Bed of Roses.
Made by Roxanne McElroy.

Music Music. Made by Elaine Lewis, The Woodlands, TX.
Look at this extraordinary quilting design—the treble clef is stitched all over the quilt.

Choosing a Quilting Design

We are fortunate that today there are many, many different quilt designs to choose from. If you do not create your own design, books and stencils offer all the ideas and help you could want. Remember that even the simplest quilt top requires intricate quilting to make it complete. In fact, I always feel that the simpler the quilt top design, the more intricate the quilting design ought to be. I have never seen an over-quilted quilt! Remember, too, as you choose or create a design that it will take time to finish. An interesting design, though it might seem complicated at first, will hold your attention and keep you from giving up on the quilt out of boredom. The objective, after all, is to end up with a finished quilt you can be proud to call a family heirloom.

I urge you to spend as much time designing your overall quilting design as you spend designing your quilt top. And spend as much or even more time quilting than you spend with piecing or appliqué. I have seen many antique quilts where the fabric has totally rotted away and the entire quilt is held together by the seam allowances and the quilting stitches. The heavier the quilting, the more securely the layers are attached, and the longer your quilt will last. A simple rule of thumb: when in doubt, add more quilting.

A Catalog of Quilting Designs

There are many ways to mark a quilt top. The design and your confidence in yourself have a lot to do with the method you choose. In this chapter, I have provided many of the most common designs, used over the ages, noting how each is best marked onto the quilt top. Each is fairly easy to mark. Remember to consider the overall feel of your quilt before choosing a design. Remember also to test any marking utensil you choose on each fabric in your quilt to be 100 percent sure that the lines can be removed later.

When using templates, I have found that cutting them out of or gluing them to the smooth side of fine sand paper will keep them from slipping while tracing around them. When using stencils, the biggest problem is that the quilter must use a marker with a very fine point in order for it to fit the slots in the stencil. Chalk and graphite pencils seem to work best.

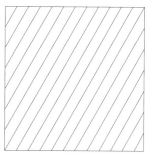

Echo-Quilting

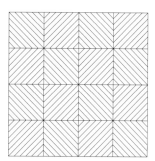

Diagonal Rays

Diagonal Rays, multiple blocks

Double Rays

Echo-Quilting

Traditional Hawaiian quilts are typically echo-quilted. This style is best suited to appliqué quilts. The quilter first quilts close to and around the edges of the appliquéd design. This is called *outline quilting*. That outline is repeated or "echoed," usually every ½″ (1 cm) until the entire surface is quilted. The distance between the lines of quilting does not always need to be ½″ (1 cm); it can vary from ¼″ to 1″ (0.5 cm to 2.5 cm), increasing as the rings move outward. Traditionally, Hawaiian quilters use the width of their thumbs as a guide. *Tiare de Tahiti* on page *xii* is echo-quilted.

Another type of echo-quilting is more symmetrical in appearance. This design is meant to look as though a pebble was thrown at the center of a pond, the ripples moving outward. The quilter draws a circle at the center of the quilt, without touching the appliqué, and quilts it. Then, at a predetermined distance, the quilter repeats larger circles until the entire quilt is quilted.

Diagonal Rays

This is an easy and convenient way to fill background areas of a quilt or quilt block. The first line is always drawn diagonally from one corner to the opposite corner with a straight edge. From there, the lines can be drawn as closely as every ¼″ (0.5 cm) or as wide apart as every 1″ (2.5 cm). Often, for convenience, quilters simply use the width of their yardsticks or rulers as a guide. The distance between the lines can drastically affect the overall feel of the quilt, so think carefully about the look you want.

Another option for quilts that have multiple blocks is to change the direction of the diagonal rays in each block. This can sometimes produce a secondary pattern. Sketch it out on paper before committing yourself to the design.

Double Rays

This quilt design is marked in the same way as diagonal rays, except that each line is accentuated by echoing it closely. Try echoing each line at ¼″ (0.5 cm), then separating each set of lines by a full 1″ (2.5 cm).

Crosshatching

Baltimore album quilts are traditionally crosshatched. Crosshatching is achieved by marking diagonal rays in one direction and then repeating them in the other direction. This produces little diamonds across the quilt. The closer the diagonal rays are placed, the more the diamonds seem to puff out in the finished product. *Annette's Bavarian Scrolls* on page 22 features crosshatching.

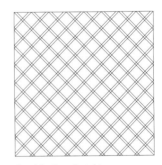

Crosshatching

Double Crosshatching

This design adds more interest. Mark double rays diagonally across the quilt and then repeat diagonally in the other direction. Double crosshatching can give a plaid look, especially when done in different colored threads. *Tahitian Hibiscus* on page 88 has a double crosshatch design. The stitches are identical in size on the front and back.

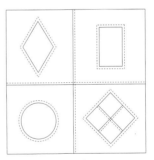

Double Crosshatching

Stitch-in-the-Ditch

Stitch-in-the-ditch is the most laborious type of quilting. The quilter simply quilts as close as possible to all the seams. It is difficult, because seam allowances come into play, requiring the quilter to wrap several layers of fabric over the needle for each stitch. To think that some teachers still recommend this design to beginners! Some quilters quilt ¼" (0.5 cm) away from each seam to avoid the hardship of seam allowances. This is fairly effective, but you usually end up quilting with the grain, which is not easy either. Still, stitching-in-the-ditch is a good way to accentuate certain areas of piecing or appliqué.

Forgetting for a moment the difficulty of stitch-in-the-ditch, consider the overall effect on the quilt. It seems to me that if a quilter has gone to the trouble of piecing together dozens of shapes, painstakingly matching the points and creating a visual line, why waste time duplicating that line? Quilting over your piecing or appliqué never covers your quilt top, it only adds to it. Actually, all the more reason to choose a completely different design to add to your top rather than duplicate it.

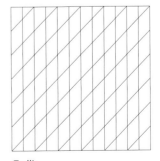

Stitch-in-the-Ditch

Trellis

This design is accomplished by marking diagonal rays from one corner of the quilt to the other, and then marking vertical or horizontal lines across the quilt. In contrast to crosshatching, the diamonds are angled in trellis.

Trellis

Double Trellis

Stippling

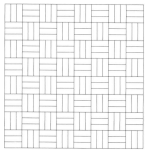

Stippling, Alternate

Stippling, Alternate

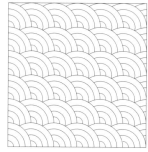

Clamshell

Double Trellis

For double trellis, first crosshatch your quilt. Then, add vertical or horizontal lines across the quilt. For a symmetrical look, make sure that each row of diamonds produced by the crosshatching (or every other one) is cut in half by a vertical or horizontal line.

Stippling

Stippling is a quilting technique in which the quilting lines are placed closely together, creating a flat but softly graded look. The look achieved can be very random or very angular. The most popular form of stippling is produced by creating a meandering line of quilting that never crosses itself but wanders over the quilt, with no less than ¾″ to ½″ (0.3 cm to 1 cm) between lines. *Shamrock Fantasy* on page 161 uses stippling.

Clamshell

This rather complicated design can be marked quite easily and can provide a fascinating effect. First, decide how far apart your quilting lines will be, and then how many layers each shell will have. Tie a string to your marking utensil. If, for example, you decide each line should be ½″ (1 cm) apart and you want each shell to have four layers, then tie four knots in your string, ½″ (1 cm) apart. Begin at one corner of the quilt top and hold the knot that is closest to your pencil down on that corner. With the string taut, place the tip of the pencil at the edge of the quilt and mark the curve until you reach the other edge. Then repeat this motion, but hold the next knot at the corner instead. This will produce a second curve ½″ (1 cm) away from the first. Repeat with the third and fourth knots. To begin the next layer of clamshells, hold the farthest knot from your pencil on the edge of your quilt where the last line you marked touches. This will become your new corner. Mark your four curves and then hold the knots at the other side of the quilt. Once you get past this point, use the intersections between last lines of clamshells as your corner to pivot your string from. You will create a pyramid effect of clamshells. The first line has one clamshell, the next line has two, and so on.

Champagne Glass

This design was traditionally marked with champagne glasses and the size of the circles is determined by the size of the glass used. First, find the center of your quilt and mark a straight line across it. Then, either tracing around a glass or using a compass, mark a row of circles along

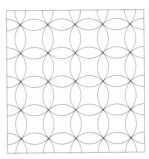

that line. You can either use the center line to match the top of the glass or have the line going down the imaginary center of the circles. Be sure to overlap each circle consistently by a predetermined amount. For the second row, overlap the circles again sideways by the same amount, and make sure the whole row overlaps the bottom row by that amount, too. When you reach the edges of the quilt and there is not enough room for an entire circle, trace the circle anyway, allowing it to run off the edges. *Balloons over New Mexico* on page *vi* uses the champagne glass design.

Champagne Glass

Too Much Champagne!

This design can provide an interesting effect to the right quilt by causing the eye to wander randomly over the quilt until the viewer discovers there is not symmetry to the pattern at all. You can do this with any geometric or even non-geometric shape. Simply trace whatever outline you choose randomly onto the quilt top, without regard to symmetry or to the number of shapes per block. Try using lollipops, a teddy bear, flowers, or candy canes. This could quickly approach a stippling design, depending on how closely you quilt.

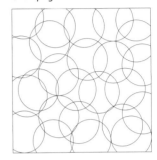

Too Much Champagne!

Outline Quilting

Not to be confused with echo-quilting or stitching-in-the-ditch, when outline quilting, the quilter takes inspiration from the fabric itself for the quilt design. If you have a dominant fabric in your quilt that has an interesting pattern, use that pattern as your template and quilt it. The advantage is that you do not have to mark the design, it is in the fabric already. Outline quilting can be quite striking when color threads are used on a white-on-white quilt. If the fabric you want to outline is not dominant, you can trace the design to create your own template and move it around randomly or in a predetermined pattern across your quilt. *Ia Orana* on page 71 is outline-quilted.

Stippling, Alternate

Feathers

Certainly one of the most elegant of all the traditional quilting designs, feathers are not nearly as difficult to mark as you might think. First, draw a line in the direction in which you wish the feathers to go. The line can be straight, curved, or a combination. Then, lay a penny against the left-hand edge of the bottom of the line. (Imagine that the 3 o'clock point on the coin is touching the line.) Trace around the penny from

Stippling, Alternate

Outline Quilting

Ted E. Bayr. Made by Dierdra A. McElroy.
This channel appliqué piece is complimented by quilting stitches
in a simple bear paw pattern.

the 12 o'clock point to the 6 o'clock point. Slide the penny upward, the 3 o'clock point still touching the directional line and the 6 o'clock point touching the top of the first feather, to stack another feather on top of the one you have drawn. Draw around the penny, line-to-line. Continue up to the top of the directional line, then repeat on the right-hand side of the line. Notice that if your line is curved the feathers on either side of it will not match up in placement.

Marking Feathers

Feathers can be quite confusing to quilt. They must be quilted in a direction that flows, as if you are drawing them, or the end product will look unnatural or even sloppy. Start at the bottom inside line of the feather. Work up, out, and around the first and second feather until you come to an intersection. Then, insert the needle between the layers and jump over to the third feather above the one you just finished, starting again at the bottom. Quilt down and around the feather to the next intersection. Then jump through the layers diagonally to the next feather. Continue until the pattern is finished.

Trapunto

Trapunto is a technique that adds dimension to specific areas of a quilt. Traditionally, a surgery-like procedure was performed on a finished quilt, whereby the back was opened up so that extra stuffing could be inserted, creating hills and valleys in the quilt. Many less invasive ways to achieve the same effect have since been developed. Some quilters use batting, others yarn or stuffing for trapunto. *Star of the Blue Grass* on page 120 and *Shamrock Fantasy* on page 161 are both excellent examples of trapunto.

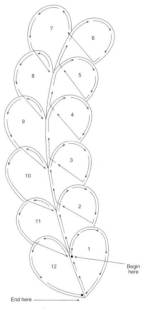

Quilting Feathers

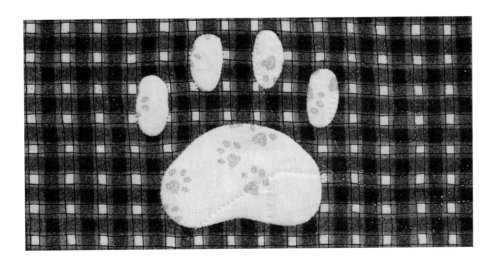

Rose

Leaf

Vines

Thorns

A Quick Start to Creating Your Own Quilting Designs

It is not difficult to design a unique and interesting background quilting design. It does not take a lot of artistic talent either. One of the easiest ways of starting your own design is to look around for a shape or a subject that interests you or that is related to your quilt. Then simply trace it onto your quilt top. I created the design of *Wedding Rings and Champagne Bubbles on a Bed of Roses* on page 32 this way. It is far less complicated than it looks.

First, I traced an image of a rose at random several times on a very large sheet of tracing paper—36″ × 36″ (90 cm × 90 cm). I flipped the paper over several times to give the rose image a slightly different look. I also varied the shapes of the petals each time to add variety. Next, I did the same with a leaf. Notice that they lie close to, but not touching, the traced roses. I took care, too, that they were not in identical positions around the roses, for a more natural look. The most demanding part of this design was to come up with a couple of vine shapes that pleased me. I placed the vines in the largest spaces between the roses. Last, I quilted thorns—since no marriage is without them!

If you decide to create a floral design like this, remember that there really are no rules. You can trace the rose in whatever size you want, you can turn it over and over again to vary the position; you can place the leaves and vines wherever you like them; and you can alter the sizes of any of the images to fit the spaces on your quilt. You can fill in empty spaces with whatever shapes or images you want. Fill an 8½″ × 11″ (210 cm × 280 cm) sheet of paper with your design.

Once the paper is full, start tracing onto the quilt. As you work on different areas of the quilt top, move the paper around to give the quilting design a more natural, random look. If your quilt top is light in color, it is easiest to place the paper behind the top and trace the design with a quality chalk pencil. Then, sandwich the quilt and baste it, or put it into the quilt frame. If your quilt top is dark in color, you may need to create a plastic stencil of your design to mark through.

Design ideas are everywhere. I often find inspiration in children's coloring books. Other places I have looked are field guides on birds, flowers, or animals. I even found a marvelous Victorian-style design in a book on wrought-iron architecture. Remember that all you need is a set of lines to follow, so any object or pattern can be reproduced in a line drawing and then quilted.

When you begin choosing or designing your own quilting design, the key is to explore the possibilities offered by the overall theme and pattern of the quilt. When you first plan your quilt and while you work on fabric selection, piecing, or appliqué, think about the quilting design. Try to find a design that is completely in tune with the feel of the quilt. If your quilt top is made of pretty floral fabrics, you may choose a subtle, elegant design. But it's much more creative to design a boy's quilt with quilted sports equipment and untied shoes with very long shoestrings as filler design than to do a trite crosshatch. The idea is to experiment. Let your imagination run free, doodle a little, and look for ideas wherever you go. You'll enjoy it—and your quilt will have a design like no other!

Quilter's Workshop

1. On a sheet of 8½″ × 11″ (210 cm × 280 cm) paper, create a quilting design for a baby or holiday quilt. Begin by making a list of items associated with babies, such as bottles, bears, blocks, and bibs. For a holiday quilt, examples might be candy canes, gingerbread men, flags, hearts, or birthday candles. Next, evaluate each object for its overall outline shape. Is it recognizable by outlines alone? Perhaps more than one object would be fun, with a "filler" in between them. Save this paper for future reference— you never know when you may need it!

2. On a sheet of 8½″ × 11″ (210 cm × 280 cm) paper, practice rotating and flipping a design to fill the paper, as if it were the quilt you were marking. Basic shapes such as oddly shaped triangles, hexagons, or uneven parallelograms can be used. Also try more complex shapes, such as flowers, trees, teddy bears, or candy canes. Save everything you finish for future use. The whole sheet of paper can become your pattern, repeating across the quilt.

CHAPTER TWELVE

Taking Care of Handmade Quilts

A quilter's greatest accomplishment is not to design a wonderful quilt, but to finish it. With hand quilting, where so many hours are invested in making all those perfect stitches, there is no greater joy or reward for the quilter than to finish her quilt. I think the reason that fine antique quilts are so highly prized is that not only do we admire the art of the creator, but we respect the amount of time she dedicated to her work. Since handmade quilts have so much thought, care, money, and time invested in them, it is important that once finished they are treated well. To make a quilt a true heirloom, both the quilter and those who inherit it from her must take the best possible care of it and so expand its life span.

Grandma's Ferns and Blackberry Pie. Made by Martha A. Nordstrand, Surprise, AZ. *Hand appliqué, hand piecing and hand-embellished—see the beads that form the blackberries! There is even hand embroidery on the leaves. A simple quilting design of leaves and vines compliments the appliqué.*

Earth's Hidden Secrets. Made by Martha A. Nordstrand.

Here, the quilting mimics the design of the appliqué stems and leaves.

Photograph by Sharon Hoogstraten

Do I Have to Wash a Hand-Made Quilt?

When all the work is done, it is natural to want to protect your hand-made quilt vigorously. Washing a quilt can be scary, given all the horror stories posted on the Internet. You can sew a label to the back of the quilt that states, "Wash this quilt over my dead body!" but I am afraid that is exactly what will happen. When children and grandchildren inherit a prized quilt that has been stored for years, it is almost always washed right away. Today we value our quilts tremendously and they are stored or used with much more care than the quilts of yesterday. While they may not need to be laundered as frequently as quilts that are slept under nightly, they do need periodic cleanings. The first and most important time is right after completion. Since the quilt is handmade, that means hands were all over it for the nine months or so it took to complete. (Okay, for some us that's more like nine years!) Think of the finger oils, house dust, pet dander, and other environmental dirt that has touched your quilt. On top of that, the quilt probably endured some stretching during its completion. It may have been stretched in the quilt frame or hoop, a pet may have slept on the corner while it was draped during quilting, or it may have been sat upon or stretched when folded. Washing allows the fabric fibers to spring back to the way they were woven, squaring up the quilt and removing oils and dirt accumulated during construction.

Art quilts are frequently an exception to the rules that all quilts need to be washed. Many art quilts are made with fibers and embellishments that would be permanently altered if they came into contact with soap and water or were agitated in a washing machine. A few fabrics, such as polished cottons, offer the quilter a unique sheen that provides an aesthetic appearance that normal fabrics can't duplicate. However, the heat treatment that is used to get that sheen is lost when the quilt is washed. Only you can know if there is something special you used in your quilt that might lose its special properties when the quilt is washed.

A Quilter's Journal

Every scientist knows that you must document every step of an experiment in order to ascertain the facts about an outcome. This is the most valuable piece of advice I can give quilters, whether they quilt by hand or machine. Keep a journal of quilt making. Whether it's a computer document or a handwritten record jotted into a pretty book or an ugly steno notebook, it doesn't matter. Just make sure you document everything about each quilt you make. Some of the decisions we make about our quilts are agonizing and take a long time, but once the decision is made we frequently forget what we chose in the end. Here are some of the things you should document:

It should come as no surprise that the best way to store a quilt is to lay it flat on a bed. I have a friend who is a prolific quilter and she frequently invites people into the guest room to view her quilts. It is very pleasant to stand there while she peels back the quilts one by one. Keeping quilts spread on a bed in this way prevents fold lines, which eventually will become stress points, causing the quilt to deteriorate.

- The fabric type and brand, including where it was purchased and how much it cost. Don't forget the backing fabric.

- What happened during prewashing of fabrics: the water temperature, the type of soap, use of bleach or fabric softeners, whether prewashing was by hand or machine, any noticeable bleeding.

- If you made or dyed the fabric yourself, document supplies and methods used.

- Brand name and type of threads; number of spools used and cost per spool; treatment of thread with beeswax, Thread Haven, or other products.

- Batting type and brand. Note if you pre-treated in any way and the results.

- Note any accidents during the construction process, such as spilling a drink on the project and cleaning the damaged spot.

- Keep notes about patterns, designs, instructions, or inspirations.

- Document the type of needles used and any issues that arose. I even keep track of how many I used!

- Note any chemicals used on the quilt, such as starch or spray sizings.

- Document any mechanical processes used (such as the quilt frame, hoop, or lap quilting) and how the quilt was basted.

Keeping a journal may seem tedious but once you do it you will begin to see trends and patterns that you likely would have never noticed. When disasters happen, you will have a way to go back and figure out why. Many quilt appraisers believe a quilt is more valuable when documentation of the kind kept in a quilt journal is available from the creator.

Soaps Versus Detergents

Soaps and detergents are products that we all use on a daily basis without giving them a second thought. Although both of these perform the same action, which is cleansing, there is a significant difference between them. We can differentiate between them based on many factors, including ingredients, structure, chemical properties, and more.

Both soaps and detergents are considered surfactants, which means that they are washing compounds that will mix with grease and water. True soaps are generally produced with natural products (fat and lye) and require significantly less energy to produce. It is possible to make soap without any waste products left over. When washed down a drain, natural soap is completely biodegradable. These soaps tend to have a pH of 9.5 to 10, making them alkaline in nature. They are extremely effective cleansing products, free of harmful antibacterial chemicals and preservatives.

Detergents are generally made from petroleum products and surfactants. Foaming agents and alcohol are their primary composition. These chemicals have a disagreeable odor so detergents are heavily scented with cheap, synthetic, artificial fragrances. Detergents also include preservatives (parabens) and antibacterial agents, which increase their shelf life but have been implicated as the cause of allergies and skin reactions.

While soaps are more environmentally friendly and less harsh on your quilts than detergents, there is another factor for quilters to consider. If you have hard water in your house, soap will produce insoluble compounds that appear as a sticky scum on your fabric! The development of synthetic detergents by chemists was a huge advantage for people with hard tap water in their homes.

For my quilts, I prefer a detergent, but it must be free of perfumes, phosphates, and dyes. In the United States detergents are now required by law to be free of phosphorous due to its proven damage to natural waterways and danger to plants and animals. I am very wary of detergents that have whiteners, fabric softeners, or other special features that may leave unwanted chemicals in the fabric.

Temperature of Water

Since soaps and detergents are both chemicals, they sit around in their bottles on the supermarket shelf in an inert form. They require something to act as a catalyst and tell it when it is time to do its job. That catalyst is the temperature of the water. Detergent manufacturers define cold water as 80 to 85 degrees Fahrenheit (27-30 Celsius), which is the temperature of the lagoon water in Tahiti where I grew up. Not exactly what I would call cold! More than likely, the water in your house pipes is lower than 80 degrees Fahrenheit or 27 degrees Celsius (unless you live in summertime Arizona!). Soaps and detergents won't activate in temperatures below 80 degrees Fahrenheit (27 degrees Celsius), not even the new cold water versions. It is always best to wash in warm water for maximum efficiency.

A Word About Fabric Softeners

Fabric softeners are designed to coat the surface of cloth fibers with a thin layer of chemicals that have lubricant properties. These chemicals make your fabric feel smoother and help prevent static electricity because they are electrically conductive. The manufacturers also claim that their products make fabrics easier to iron and more resistant to stains, wrinkling, and pilling. Really good quality fabrics don't need chemical fabric softeners because with repeated washings and drying they become softer naturally.

One of the benefits of keeping a journal of your quilt making is that if something horrible happens, you can go back and track issues with some measure of sureness. Over the past twenty years I have been able to ascertain that certain marking utensils can react with the chemicals in fabric softeners. This reaction can cause the normally temporary marks to become quite permanent, destroying the quilt! If you are a big fan of using fabric softeners for their obvious soft and fragrant properties, you might consider foregoing their use until after the quilt is completed.

Hand Washing Versus Machine Washing

Today's machines are absolutely amazing. If you have a front-load, high-energy machine with a hand wash or delicate cycle, then use it for your quilts. These machines can be much more gentle than our hands in a bathtub or sink. The machines are designed to remove the maximum amount of moisture from the quilt without having to wring it out, risking damage to the stitches or fabric. My Maytag Neptune can handle a queen size quilt nicely, where I used to go through quite a tedious process to wash my larger quilts. I used to scrub my bathtub sparkling clean then fill it to a few inches with warm water. I had a brand new toilet plunger that was marked 'quilts only'. After adding a few drops of detergent, I would lay out the quilt and agitate gently with the plunger. Detergent breaks down oils and dirt but agitation separates them from the fabric so the water can wash the grime away. I would then drain the bathtub, plunge the excess water out of the quilt, and refill the tub for rinsing. When the quilt was washed and as much excess water as possible squished out, the quilt would get wrapped in a towel and carried outside where it was gently laid out on a sheet. Another sheet was then spread across it to prevent the sun access to my art.

These days I also dry my quilts in the dryer. My washing machine leaves the quilt practically dry so there is not much drying needed. Still, I put the quilts in the dryer on a gentle cycle with lower heat and monitor the dryer carefully. Most of the damage in the dryer will occur from leaving a quilt in there for too long; the dryer can overheat and scorch cotton materials or damage dyes, causing colors to fade. Another factor to think about when considering using a machine to dry your quilts: children. Make absolute sure there is no chance of a stray crayon, piece of candy, or lip gloss left in the dryer from a load of clothing. This can destroy a quilt in a matter of seconds!

Ironing Quilts

Many quilters are obsessed with ironing their fabrics and their quilts. There are times that ironing is necessary during the construction process. It has to be done correctly and carefully to avoid damaging the fibers of the fabric. Avoid ironing unless absolutely necessary. If you must iron, keep the iron moving so that heat does not build up to extreme temperature in any one spot.

There are several sprays available to aid in getting wrinkles out of fabric. I avoid starch sprays because the chemicals in them attract moths and other bugs. Spray-sizing seems to work quite well; it reduces ironing time and doesn't leave the fabric stiff. In fact, spray-sizing can make fabric feel much like it did at the quilt shop when I bought it. Be aware that anything you spray on your fabric is a chemical that will stay on the surface and very possibly could interact with whatever marking tool you will be using. Ironing already quilted quilts will just flatten the loft in the quilt. Fold lines in quilts have a way of becoming very stubborn and appear to be permanent, although I have found that hanging the quilt and using a clothing steamer will get fold lines out.

Storing Quilts

Ask a dozen quilters how they store their quilts and you will get as many answers. The choices you make for storing your quilts will depend on your lifestyle and personal preference. One of the most common is to spread quilts out on top of each other on a bed in a guest bedroom that is not used. This avoids stubborn fold marks; if a plain sheet is draped over the top quilt you won't have to worry about sun from the window or dust settling.

Most quilters I know keep at least a couple of quilts folded over a quilt display rack somewhere in the house. They keep them out of the sun and refold periodically in different way to avoid permanent wrinkles. If you are storing your quilts in a cupboard or closet, be aware that the natural acids in the wood of shelving and drawers can damage the fibers of a quilt over the long term. Instead, line the shelves with acid-free paper before folding the quilts and placing them in storage.

Many quilters have taken to sewing pillow cases to store their quilts in. A zipper one end ensures that the quilt is protected yet the fibers can still breathe. If your quilts get shipped for display at quilt shows or to be photographed, a pillow case is a great way to protect them.

Displaying Quilts

Direct sunlight is ruinous to fiber, and quilts should never be placed on a bed or hung on a wall that is in sunlight. If you are considering displaying an heirloom quilt on a bed, observe that bed at various times of day throughout the year to ensure that the sun never directly touches it. Before you decide to display a quilt, consider the climate in which you live, too—humidity causes quilts to deteriorate more quickly.

When hanging a quilt, make sure the quilt has equal support all along the hanging edge. The best way to do this is to make a quilt sleeve to apply to the back of the quilt. Cut a strip of fabric 8" (20 cm) wide and as long as the quilt is wide. Hem the two short edges of the strip, then fold the strip in half lengthwise and sew the long edge together to form a tube. Flatten the tube and tack it securely to the top edge of the quilt with an appliqué stitch. Make sure your stitches don't show to the front of the quilt. Insert a pole through the quilt sleeve and hang it on the wall to be admired by all who visit! Be careful that the sun will not change angles as the seasons change and touch your quilt for even a few minutes each day. Quilts should not be hung directly over or under heating ducts as the constant flow of hot air will damage the fibers.

There are a large variety of wooden hanging systems for wall quilts on the market. Question the manufacturer about their use of stains and varnishes to be sure that they have chosen the correct ones with quilts in mind. Some of those products could leach acids or fumes into your quilt if haphazardly done. A nice wooden display with spotlights inserted can provide an amazingly elegant way to display your art in your home!

Transporting Quilts

I have consulted many quilters about shipping methods. I hand carry all of my quilts with me to shows or guilds where I will be presenting. I have learned a couple of harsh lessons though, such as suitcases do get left on the tarmac in pouring rain. So I put my quilts inside clean trash bags and then load them into the suitcases. My suitcases are now also chosen for water resistance.

If you have to ship a quilt, use expedited service, such as Next Day Air or Three Day Select with UPS, rather than less expensive ground service. With expedited services, the box gets handled less, with fewer chances of it getting misdirected or mislaid. Require a signature upon delivery so that a box of valuable quilts is not left on a doorstep. Package the quilt in a fabric bag and then inside a plastic bag before boxing it up. This will protect it from any adverse weather conditions. I also tend to put an extra layer of cardboard over and under the quilt and some sort of padding to protect against punctures or slips of the box cutter while opening. I know a few art quilters who ship their quilts rolled and placed in tubes almost as tall as they are to avoid wrinkles settling in before hanging at major shows. It is up to each quilter to decide about insurance. UPS automatically insures every package for $100. Unless you are willing to accept that in the rare instance of loss or damage, then you should insure the quilt for a figure closer to its value

Labeling Quilts

There are as many good reasons to label your quilts as there are creative ways to label them. Quilt shows require quilts to be labeled for easy identification. It also makes sense to label in case a quilt is lost, misplaced or stolen. Just as importantly, however, you should label your quilts for the sake of posterity. One day, one of your descendants will recognize the beauty of your quilt and wonder at its history.

To label a quilt, simply write your name, the name of the quilt, year completed, and other information you would like to share onto a piece of fabric and sew it onto a corner of the backing. Some artists are quite creative with their labels. I have seen labels shaped like flowers, teddy bears, or butterflies. Some quilters appliqué intricate designs around their label to reflect the overall theme on the front of the quilt or embroider their information to the label. Artists who are accomplished at photo transfers enjoy creating personalized labels with their own portraits or with pictures that inspired their quilts. Your quilt might be lucky enough to last 200 years or more—label it so that you, as well as your perfect stitches, are remembered!

Quilt Appraisals

I cannot stress enough the importance of having your quilts appraised. A certified quilt appraiser documents all the vital information about your quilt, such as the maker(s), dates, size, design, inspiration, materials, and so on. An appraiser will usually take pictures and record any history that you can relate. As a result of the appraisal, an "insurance appraisal amount" will be assigned to your quilt. In a worst case scenario, if something happens to your cherished quilt an insurance company will only settle for basic cost of materials. If the value of the quilt can be substantiated with a certified appraisal it will go a long way towards helping you recover from a very difficult situation.

Quilt appraisers are frequently historians and they are uniquely qualified to help you date an antique quilt that you have discovered. Their knowledge and expertise can help guide decisions about repairs or finishing tops that have been inherited. They have a wealth of knowledge overall and their nominal fee is more than worth a good evaluation.

Questions and Answers

Thinking back over my years of teaching the quilting stitch, I have collected a sampling of the most frequently asked questions. The type of person who is drawn to hand quilting seems to have a perfectionist tendency and is always searching to achieve That Perfect Stitch. Never forget that as the artist you have personally placed every single stitch into your quilt and can see minor flaws. Do not berate yourself too strongly for what you may consider unevenness. Enlist the opinions of other quilters or stand back from your quilt to get an overall look. Separate yourself from the individual stitches. If you still see a problem, refer to the questions that follow. Happy quilting!

*The quilt behind is the backing of **Mermaids in the Surf** (see page 17).
The quilt in front is **Scottish Thistle** (see page 156). Above is a name label
from **Tricycles and Trains** (see page 46).*

Q. How can I stop my needle from slipping off the thimble?

A. Make sure that as you rotate the needle, you are keeping the eye at a 90 degree angle and are not merely shoving the needle flat backwards. Also make sure that your thimble has dimples that are deep enough to hold the needle. Check this by holding the needle and placing it in a dimple. Then try to move it around. The needle should not budge sideways across the thimble easily, if at all. If you have determined that the dimples are indeed deep enough and the needle still slips out, it is most likely because the thimble is not being rotated slightly to keep the needle at a 90° angle inside the dimple (see page 63). No matter how deep the dimples are, if you do not keep the thimble in contact with the needle, it will slip out of the dimple.

Q. Why are my stitches underneath the quilt much smaller than those on top?

A. This can be caused by one of two things. The most common cause is that the quilter does not rotate the needle back up to a 90° angle after every stitch. The needle must penetrate all three layers of the quilt at a perpendicular angle in order for the stitches on top to match those on the bottom.

Another cause that some quilters encounter is that their fingers are just too sensitive. For these unlucky few, the finger underneath the quilt feels the top of the needle as it penetrates the layers so quickly that they stop pushing and return the tip to the surface a little too early. During the rotation, they drop a thread or two off the needle, causing smaller stitches or missing stitches altogether. To correct the problem, the quilter must feel the needle come through the fabric slightly farther before stopping and returning to the surface. The only solution is to toughen up the finger. Quilters who tolerate the discomfort for short periods at a time will develop a quilter's callus on the finger which will be a natural barrier and solve the problem. Let's be clear here. I am not saying you should tolerate pain, and certainly bleeding is completely unacceptable. You can try using New Skin before quilting. This will add an extra layer of protection. See Chapter 8 for other helpful aids that will protect the finger.

There are devices made for underneath the quilt. I usually do not recommend them, because a high degree of sensitivity underneath the quilt is necessary for That Perfect Stitch. However, those with extra-sensitive fingers need something. I provide Thimble-Its to my students in class. They are oval disks that let you sense the needle but provide a tough layer that does not puncture easily. Medical wraps do not work as successfully, due to their porous nature. It is difficult to judge the distance that the needle has protruded with anything on the finger, so if you do use a finger protector, go slowly so that you can better judge how far the needle has gone.

Q. My stitches on top of the quilt are huge. Why?

A. Using the rocking system, this problem almost always occurs because the quilter accidentally pushes on the needle while trying to rotate it back up to a 90° angle. Instead of pushing, the needle should be caught gently in a dimple in the thimble and simply rotated. It should not advance through the fabric at all yet. It takes a quick wrist movement to go from laying flat to standing upright. This takes some practice and will come as the quilter gains control.

Q. Why are my stitches much larger on the back of the quilt than on the top?

A. You are allowing your needle to slip through the layers of the quilt as you rotate the needle down. Strive to achieve a very definite rotate *or* push. Do not do both at the same time. As you rotate, the needle should be gently caught in a dimple and you should be able to manipulate the angle. Your underneath finger should be pushing up exactly below the needle's point. Make sure you are not inadvertently pushing the needle. The bottom finger will know if you are pushing by sending a pain signal to your brain! With a good thimble, you should not need to use your thumb to hold it in place. A finger *and* a thumb on the thimble makes it hard to control, whether you are pushing or just rotating.

Q. Why is my first stitch in each series always larger than the rest?

A. Unfortunately, this is the case for most of us. If I have not quilted in a few days, I experience the same problem. Therefore, I never knot my thread until I have warmed up for a few minutes. For beginners, this will continue to be a problem for a few hours of total quilting time. It is purely a matter of balance and control, since there is nothing holding the needle yet. To achieve control, stick the needle into the quilt by half its length at the point at which you want to begin stitching. Place the index finger of the underneath hand on the tip of the needle that is protruding below. Place the thimble on the eye of the needle. Obviously, at this point, if either finger pushes on the needle, the other finger will suffer. Gently hold the needle between the two fingers and move them in tandem upward until the bottom finger can tell that the needle is barely penetrating the fabric layers. There should be pressure on the quilt surface, causing a "mountain" of fabric. I usually have to put more pressure on the fabric during the first stitch than the second or third. The tightening of the fabric fibers around the needle will help hold it in place. Begin pivoting down and back, going into your first stitch. Pivot, do not push down on the needle, or you will chew up the skin of the bottom finger, as well as cause your bottom stitches to be larger than the top ones.

Q. Why does my needle keep popping out of the fabric as I begin to pivot?

A. This only happens on the first of a series of stitches, and it is because nothing is holding the needle down yet. Sometimes the needle pops because the underneath finger drops a little, loosening the quilt slightly and allowing the needle to fall over or pop. Instead of putting the needle in at the recommended 90° angle, try inserting it into the quilt angled slightly toward you. This should stop the popping. Also, try not to put so much pressure on the needle with your thimble at this point. As you learn to control the needle, this problem should disappear.

Q. Though I feel in control of my stitches, they are still uneven. Why?

A. One cause could be that when you use your thumb in front of the needle point, as it resurfaces from below, you are facing the pad of the thumb to the point. You should not use the thumb pad to feel for the needle to resurface. Your vision is more acute than your sense of touch, and using the thumb in this manner blocks your vision. With time, as the needle keeps touching the thumb pad, even if it touches softly and without pain, the skin builds up a callus. The callus makes your thumb less sensitive, causing your stitches to be larger and more uneven as you wait to feel the needle come through. Rotate your wrist slightly in toward your body and make sure you are quilting south, toward yourself. This will position your thumb in a manner that will allow you to flatten it in front of the needle tip. The needle should then resurface above your thumb. Keep in mind that if you use the pad of the thumb and slip while pushing the needle, you could hurt yourself.

Another cause of unevenness is that the quilting lines are not quite straight. Each stitch seems to march to the beat of a different drummer. When quilting along straight lines, a good way to avoid this problem is to make sure that when you pivot the needle down and back, it lays along the quilting line and not slightly off to one side. Then, push on the needle to penetrate the layers and make the stitch. When quilting curves, make sure the tip is definitely resurfacing on the quilting line. It is critical to have good lighting when quilting. The extreme tip of the needle is so sharp and fine, it is nearly impossible to see. A good strong light shining over the shoulder opposite your top hand should help you avoid shadows cast by the hand. It will make the very tip of the needle glint, helping you to spot it more quickly, thereby better controlling the stitch.

Q. Why do I get shoulder and hand cramps, even when I quilt for very short periods of time?

A. First, consult a doctor if you consistently feel pain. Once your doctor has cleared you of any serious medical conditions, take a careful study of your posture as you quilt. Where do you sit? How do you sit? What technique do you use? A quilter in good health should be able to quilt all day, with the eyes tiring first. Avoid sitting stark upright. Instead, relax in a chair with back support, placing a pillow in the small of your back for added support. If you are sitting at a frame, use a swivel chair with good lumbar support. Rather than twisting your wrists, neck or shoulders to follow a quilting line, turn your body so that you are in a better position to follow the lines. I like to quilt with a knee up to support my hoop, so I have a footstool. Place your quilt hoop in your lap. Before you begin quilting, take time to relax. Release all tension, let your shoulders fall, and let your arms rest at your sides. Take a deep breath. Your shoulders should be down, elbows resting against your sides, and wrists only slightly bent toward your body. The fingers and thumb should also be toward your lap, forming a backward letter *C*. This is the correct quilting position. The only adjustments to be made are to lift your arm and bend the elbow more in order to position your hand over your hoop. The shoulders remain down, wrists relaxed. Remember always to quilt south or toward yourself, if you can. This is the most natural and relaxed direction possible. This is especially important for people with arthritis. Any other direction will only aggravate the condition with time.

Q. Why do my needles constantly bend and break as I quilt?

A. A certain amount of bending is to be expected. A lot of stress is placed on our needles while creating That Perfect Stitch. Needles should not snap before they bend, so, first, make sure you are using a quality needle (see Chapter 3). If your needle bends every few stitches, you should re-evaluate the conditions under which you are quilting. What fabrics and battings are you working with? If they pose several compromises as discussed in Chapters 1 and 2, you should use a needle that is stronger to handle the pressure. Accept that it may not be possible to obtain as tiny a stitch as you are used to on this particular project. Focus on evenness, instead. I often have to drop to a size 9 Betweens to get through seam allowances or painted fabric. Be realistic about the size of needle you are using—use the one that it takes to get the job done well, not the smallest one possible.

Q. *Is quilting like riding a bicycle, you never forget how?*

A. Well, sort of. Once you get the hang of it, you will most likely always remember the principles behind the technique. However, like riding a bike, if you have not done it in a while, it takes a little practice to get back into the swing of things. I tell my students that learning to quilt is like learning to play the piano—you must practice daily for at least 15 minutes. I even offer to write them notes to take home so that their families will leave them alone!

Q. *Why does my thread constantly knot up on me?*

A. First, make sure that you are using a heavily waxed thread, such as Gutermann or YLI. This will help to a certain degree. Another important reason for knotting, however, is that the quilter unknowingly rolls the needle between the thumb and finger toward her body as she pulls the thread through the quilt. After a few times, the thread twists and tangles, and eventually forms knots. To counteract this, I trained myself consciously to roll the needle one turn away from my body every time I pulled the thread through after a series of stitches. This stopped the problem completely.

Q. *Should I be concerned about copyrights on quilting designs I use?*

A. Make sure that the designs you use are not copyright protected. The symbol ©, followed by a name, indicates copyright. Copyright laws are intended to prevent anyone from using an intellectual property, such as a quilting design, for profit. There is a fine line between using a copyrighted design for inspiration and plagiarizing that design. When in doubt, do not use a design without permission. Remember, it is illegal to photocopy a page or pattern from a book that is protected by copyright, even if you are just sending it to a friend because she does not want to buy the whole book. If you wish to enter competitions, be published, or produce patterns, you must obtain written permission from the copyright holder first. If you are making a quilt purely for your own enjoyment and use, there is no need to worry about copyright.

Your own original designs can be copyrighted to prevent others from using them for profit, and I recommend that you copyright your designs, even if you do not think of them as works of art. Copyright laws are complicated, so enlist the services of an intellectual property attorney to help you.

Q. How do I know when I am ready to enter a quilt show?

A. When you have finished a quilt! I encourage all quilters to enter shows. It can be so thrilling if you go into it with the right attitude. True quilt art is creating what you feel, what turns you on, what makes you happy. Displaying your quilt in a show is the culmination of all the work, a wonderful way to celebrate a major accomplishment. In addition, you get to see the judges' opinions of your quilt, and can listen while show-goers view it, without them knowing you are there! If you have an open mind and take it with a grain of salt, this is the best free advice you could ever get on your quilting. Never enter a show with high hopes of winning. Judging is extremely personal and there are no set guidelines for an award-winning quilt. Do not ever let a judge's comments discourage you from creating a new quilt or completing an existing one.

Lesson Plan

Τhat Perfect Stitch is a nationally renowned quilting class that I have been teaching for several years. Students learn the quantifiable reasons why products work for or against us while we quilt and how to evaluate these products on their own in the future. Breaking down the technique into very distinct steps ensures that each and every student will succeed to the best of his or her ability. I always have at least two students leave the class quilting as nicely as I do, and they only get 45 minutes to one hour of actual quilting time in a three-hour class. Be patient. Describe the process in as many different ways as possible. Some students learn best by reading, others by seeing, and still others by hearing. Cover all three approaches in your class.

Jewell's Paradise. Made by Roxanne McElroy.
The circles radiating out from the center draw the eye to the border of the quilt which is echo-quilted, with hibiscus blossoms in relief.

Skill Level: Beginner to intermediate

Duration: Six hours, broken up into two three-hour sessions or three two-hours sessions

Size: As space allows. Each student needs a chair and enough table space to lay out the project flat for basting.

First Hour

Chapters 1 and 2 of *That Perfect Stitch*

Explain that fabric is woven to the warp and to the weft, and introduce the concept of stitches per inch (cm). Show samples of different types of fabric—muslin, batiks, hand-dyed, painted, etc., paying special attention to the weave of each. Explain the effect on the stitch of quilting with each fabric type, showing samples prepared before class, if you can. Review prewashing of fabric. Discuss battings, reviewing fiber types, loft, bearding, and the effect of batting type on the quilting stitch. Show quilts made from various batting types, or show samples you prepared before class.

Second Hour

Chapters 3, 4, and 5 of *That Perfect Stitch*

Explain the knap of thread and show samples of different brands. Explain how needles are made, so that students understand the importance of using high-quality needles to achieve That Perfect Stitch. Pass a magnifying lens around the class so that students can see the difference between good and bad needles. Emphasize that the smallest needle is not always the best one to use. Have students try on a variety of thimbles to find the size and brand that is right for them. Discuss each thimble's purpose, unique features, and disadvantages. Explain that quilting causes an enormous amount of stress on the finger, demonstrating how the thimble is used.

Third Hour

Chapters 6, 7, and 8 of *That Perfect Stitch*

Review frames and hoops, referring students to the Resources at the back of the book for information on specific brands. Have students baste their projects as you walk around the room. Demonstrate how to place the quilt in a hoop, showing how to adjust on the warp and weft, never pulling on the bias. Show samples of different markers on sample "quilt sandwiches." Prepare in advance samples that have been washed and ironed to show the damage to fibers. Review the helpful aids in Chapter 8. Mention quilting designs and the importance of choosing a design that complements the quilt top.

Fourth to Sixth Hours
Chapter 9 of *That Perfect Stitch*

Demonstrate the quilter's knot, emphasizing that when done correctly, the knot is resistant to coming undone inside the quilt. In small groups, demonstrate how to begin the first stitch, while the rest of the class listens. Make your explanation as clear as possible, changing the way you express it so that everyone understands.

Again in small groups, demonstrate the quilting stitch. Give ideas on how to balance the needle on that first stitch. Then, slowly manipulate your needle, describing what you are doing. Tell students when to push and when not to push. Explain the importance of rotation and the role of the thumb. Avoid using the words *left hand* and *right hand*; instead talk about the *upper hand* and *underneath hand*. Have students try out the stitch, waiting a few minutes to give them time to get started before you watch them. Correct only one thing at a time, giving them a chance to understand and work on the correction before offering any further help. As students come near the end of their thread, demonstrate how to knot-off.

Be patient and completely confident that they *will* all succeed! Some students take longer than others, some have physical problems that impede their immediate progress (help them find a way around them), and still others have mental blocks from past learning experiences. It is your job to break through all barriers one at a time and give each student confidence. (You will hear "I can't" or "my fingers won't" often. It is more talk than mental attitude. Students really want to quilt well or they would not be sitting in your class. Let them say it, but do not give up on them or get frustrated. They can do it!)

During the last half-hour, share the chart showing stitches per inch (cm). Measure each student's work, showing how each has improved over the session.

Finally, discuss how quilts are valued. Encourage students to continue practicing. Mention any quilt shows coming up in the area and encourage them to attend. Above all, remind them that if they are having any difficulties working on a particular quilt to take a good look at the elements in that quilt before they assume it's their own fault. Usually, the tools they are using are to blame!

Resources

The following names and addresses are provided because it is often useful to contact manufacturers directly when you experience problems with or have questions about a quilting product. Many, if not all, of these companies have Research & Development departments that can address your concerns. The manufacturer can also direct you to local stores that carry their products. Alternatively, ask your quilt shop to order items for you. They are usually very receptive to new products and try to meet their customers' needs. Several manufacturers and publishers also have Web pages, where you can discover interesting information on new products and services for quilters.

Scottish Thistle. Made by Roxanne McElroy.
Quilting along the dividing lines of plaid fabric can give the illusion of a pieced background.

Quilting Tools and Materials

FABRIC

Alexander Henry Fabrics
1120 Scott Road
Burbank, CA 91504

Bali Fabrications
21787 8th Street E, Suite 1
Sonoma, CA 95476

Concord House
1359 Broadway
New York, NY 10018

Hoffman California Fabrics
25792 Obrero Drive
Mission Viejo, CA 92691

Kona Bay Fabrics
1637 Kahai Street
Honolulu, HI 96819

Marcus Brothers Fabrics
980 Avenue of the Americas
New York, NY 10018

Maywood Studios
6000 N. Cutter Circle,
Portland, OR 97217

Moda Fabrics
13800 Hutton Drive
Dallas, TX 75234

P & B Textiles
1580 Gilbreth Road
Burlingame, CA 94010

Peter Pan Fabrics
1071 6th Avenue
New York, NY 10018

RJR Fashion Fabrics
2203 Dominguez Street
Building K-3
Torrance, CA 90501

Robert Kaufman Fabrics
129 West 132nd Street
Los Angeles, CA 90061

South Sea Import Fabrics
550 West Artesia Boulevard
Compton, CA 90220

V.I.P. Fabrics
1412 Broadway
New York, NY 10018

BATTING

Fairfield Processing Corp.
PO Box 1157
Danbury, CT 06810

Hobb's Bonded Fibers
PO Box 2521
Waco, TX 78708-2521

Mountain Mist/The Stearns Technical Textiles
2551 Crescentville Road
Cincinnati, OH 45241

Quilter's Dream Batting
589 Central Drive
Virginia Beach, VA 23454

The Warm Company
5529 186th Place SW
Lynwood, WA 98037

NEEDLES

Bohin France
BP 212 Saint Sulpice sur Risle
61300 Laigle, Normandy, France
www.bohin.fr

Clover Needlecraft
1007 East Monguex Street
#L Carson, CA 90746

Colonial Needle Co.
74 Westmoreland Ave
White Plains, NY 10606

Wright
85 South Street
West Warren, MA 01092
(Boye Needles)

THREAD

Aurifil Thread
500 N. Michigan Ave, Suite 300
Chicago, IL 60611

Coats & Clark, Inc.
3430 Torringdon Way
Suite 301
Charlotte, NC 28277

DMC Corporation
775 Hackensack Avenue
Building 10F,
South Kearny, NJ 07032

Gutermann
PO Box 7387
Charlotte, NC 28241

Presencia Thread
PO Box 2409
Evergreen, CO 80437

Superior Thread Co
87 E 2580 S
St George, UT 84790

Valdana Thread
3551 199th Street,
Edmonton, Alberta
Canada T6M 2NS

YLI Thread
1439 Dave Lyle Boulevard,
#16C
Rock Hill, SC 29730

THIMBLES

Comfort Thimble
PO Box 442
Gresham, OR 97030

Roxanne's Thimble/Colonial Needle Co.
74 Westmoreland Ave,
White Plains, NY 10606

Thimbles by TJ Lane
PO Box 30595
Lincoln, NE 68503
www.thimbles2fit.com

FRAMES AND HOOPS

Edmunds Frames
6111 South Sayre
Chicago, IL 60638

Flynn Quilt Frame Co.
1000 Shiloh Overpass Road
Billings, MT 59106

Grace Frame Co.
2225 S 3200 W
Salt Lake City, UT 84119

Hinterburg
2805 E. Progress Drive
West Bend, WI 53095

Jasmine Heirlooms
50 Fairview Drive
Greenville, SC 29609

Morgan Quality Products
8040 Erie Ave.,
Chanhassen, MN 55317

Pleasant Mountain Frames
790 W. Larson
Bellingham, WA 98226

QUILTING DESIGNS

The Stencil Company
28 Castelwood Drive
Cheektowaga, NY 14227

Stensource International
18971 Hess Avenue
Sonora, CA 95370

SCISSORS

Fiskars Scissors
7811 West Stewart Avenue
Wausau, WI 54401

Gingher Scissors
PO Box 8865
Greensboro, NC 27419

Roxanne International

Roxanne International is now owned by Colonial Needle Co. Products created by Roxanne and Dierdra McElroy are available from this excellent source of needlework and quilting products, including Roxanne's Thimble and Roxanne's Quilter's Choice markers. You can reach Colonial Needle Co. at 74 Westmoreland Ave, White Plains, NY 10606 or visit www.colonialneedle.com.

To reach Dierdra McElroy regarding seminars, workshops, and tours, contact: That Perfect Stitch Seminars, 742 Granite Ave, Lathrop, CA 97330 or visit www.thatperfectstitch.com.

Other Useful Resources

HAND-DYE SUPPLIES

Pro Chemical & Dye, Inc.
PO Box 14
Somerset, MA 02726

QUILT DISPLAY SYSTEMS

Jasmine Heirlooms
50 Fairview Drive
Greenville, SC 29609

Zellerwood Originals/Display Away
PO Box 54289
Cincinnati, OH 45254

QUILT MAGAZINES

*American Patchwork &
Quilting Magazine*
1921 Grand Avenue
Des Moines, IA 50309

Leman Publications
741 Corporate Circle, Suite A
PO Box 4101
Golden, CO 80402
(*Quilter's Newsletter Magazine,
Quiltmaker Magazine, Quilts & Other
Comforts*)

Lady's Circle Patchwork Magazine
PO Box 267
Sussex, WI 53089

QUILT PUBLISHERS

Breckling Press
283 Michigan Avenue
Elmhurst, IL 60126

C & T Publishing
1851 Challenge Drive
Concord, CA 94520

That Patchwork Place
PO Box 118
Bothell, WA 98041

QUILTING ORGANIZATIONS

American Quilter's Society
PO Box 3290
Paducah, KY 42003

International Quilt Association
7660 Woodway, Suite 550
Houston, TX 77063

National Quilt Association
PO Box 393, Suite 550
Ellicott City, MD 21041

QUILT SHOWS

American Quilter's Society
PO Box 3290
Paducah, KY 42003

Mancuso Show Management
PO Box 667
New Hope, PA 18938
(Pennsylvania National Quilt
Extravaganza, Pacific International
Quilt Festival, MidAtlantic Quilt
Festival, World Quilt & Textile Show)

National Quilt Association
PO Box 393, Suite 550
Ellicott City, MD 21041

Quilts, Inc.
7660 Woodway, Suite 550
Houston, TX 77063
(International Quilt Market,
International Quilt Festival
European Quilt Market,
Quilt Expo)

Quilting Designs

Wedding Rings and Champagne Bubbles on a Bed of Roses

Vines from Wedding Rings and Champagne Bubbles on a Bed of Roses

Carousel

Hummingbirds

Heart and Rose

Tahitian Hibiscus

Philodendron

Autumn Leaves 1

Autumn Leaves 2

Autumn Leaves 3

La Coquillage (The Shell)

The Candle

Egg Basket

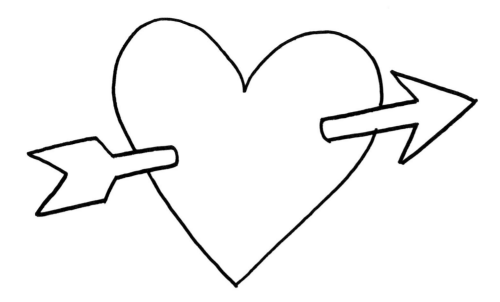

Heart

Teddy Bear

Paws

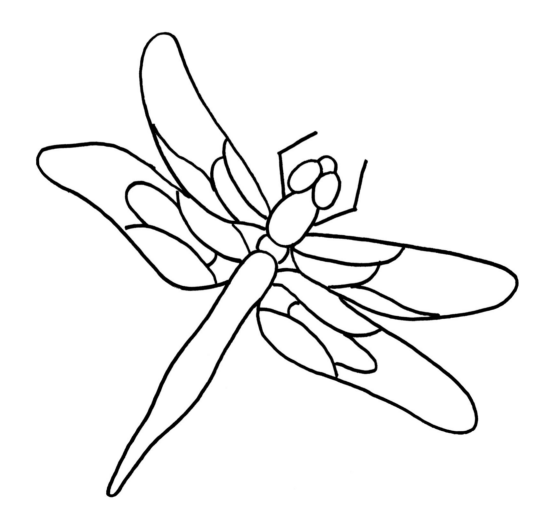

Dragonfly

Grapes

Star

Gingerbread Man

Bunny

Shamrock

Flowers

Bird of Paradise